The Chilswell Book of
English Poetry

The
Chilswell Book
of
English Poetry
compiled
& annotated for the use of schools
by
ROBERT BRIDGES
Poet Laureate

Granger Index Reprint Series

BOOKS FOR LIBRARIES PRESS
FREEPORT, NEW YORK

First Published 1924
Reprinted 1971

PR1175
B726
1971

INTERNATIONAL STANDARD BOOK NUMBER
0-8369-6294-X

LIBRARY OF CONGRESS CATALOG CARD NUMBER
74-168774

PRINTED IN THE UNITED STATES OF AMERICA
BY
NEW WORLD BOOK MANUFACTURING CO., INC.
HALLANDALE, FLORIDA 33009

DEDICATED

by gracious permission

to

H. R. H.

The PRINCE of WALES

PREFACE

I

POETRY being the most intimate expression of Man's Spirit, it is necessary to education; since no man can be a worthy citizen of any earthly state unless he be first a citizen of the heavenly.

The other fine arts aim also at spiritual expression, but their material forms are more remote from ideas, and their interpretation often requires some special disposition of mind—as in Music, wherein also the appeal, being to moods and untranslatable emotions, is uncertain of its moral effects. But in poetry the material is language, and words are not only familiar to all of us, but are of all forms the most significant that we have.

Prose, while using the same material, is no rival to poetry in this part of education; for though it be the logical guardian of Truth, and may rise to the highest pitch of expression, and—as we see in Plato, himself a poet—may duly claim the rank and name of Poetry, yet it is the common drudge of the Understanding for all work, and consequently inseparable from the usual routine of life, which is the chiefest enemy to spiritual abstraction. Poetry, on the other hand, with a more memorable form and a diction more musical, is of set purpose devoted to the high imaginative task of displaying the beauty, solemnity, and mystery of man's life on earth.

Language has a hidden but commanding influence in directing spiritual life. In whatever country we may be born, we imbibe the ideas inherent to its speech; nor can we escape from the bias which that accident must give to our minds, unless we learn other languages and study their literatures. In the physical and mathematical sciences, which can either employ precise definitions or fix the reference of their terms by sensible instances, this is not true : the signification of their corresponding terms in different languages is determinate and constant for all peoples ; but our higher aspirations and imaginative faculties, having no measure nor any objects for the senses to grasp, cannot have their expression thus standardised : the commonest names in this field of thought (such words as spirit, soul, life, reason, and mind) do not mean to us precisely what their equivalents mean in other tongues, and the inter-relations of those other meanings are consequently alien to our thoughts.

And in these higher faculties themselves there are actual differences distinguishing the different races of mankind—differences that may be ascribed to radical peculiarities of mind ; and the words which came to be coined to express them must in their currencies have reacted powerfully to strengthen those peculiar ways of thought and feeling, and to control the character of the men who used them, because our Ideals, which are formed upon habits of thought and feeling, influence and wholly prescribe our moral conduct and spiritual life.

Whence it follows that Poetry, which is made of this material, must be the expression of a nation's spirit : and English Poetry is the expression of the English Spirit in its most definite form.

Now, to speak of the English Spirit, what it is which is thus set before us, we shall not lightly underrate the heritage which has given us our high place among the nations ; but our part is to preserve it rather than to proclaim it, and to perfect it rather than to preserve it. The better our possession, the more capable is it of improvement ; and the higher we stand, the baser our defection, if we seize not the yet higher good that we stand within reach of, nor take due occasion

of our position to be an example to others ; that
being the only true national pride, since by example
only will mankind be led onward to well-being : which
example is to be manifested in the improvement of the
best, not in any extirpation or upraising of the worst,
these being the proper effects, not the causes or means
of amelioration.

II

This book is a Primer of English Poetry, and if it
differ from others of its kind, that will be because it
is unfalteringly faithful to a sound principle hitherto
insufficiently observed. While in all other Arts it is
agreed that a student should be trained only on the
best models, wherein technique and aesthetic are both
exemplary, there has been with respect to Poetry a
pestilent notion that the young should be gradually
led up to excellence through lower degrees of it ; so
that teachers have invited their pupils to learn and
admire what they expected them to outgrow : and
this was carried so far that writers, who else made no
poetic pretence, have good-naturedly composed poems
for the young, and in a technique often as inept as their
sentiment.

This mistake rested on two shallow delusions ; first,
that beauty must needs be fully apprehended before it
can be felt or admired : secondly, that the young are
unimaginative. A French writer has brushed all this
fallacy aside in a few sentences in which he tells his own
early experience.[1]

' In this little poem (he writes) there were many
words and phrases that were new to me, and which I
could not understand ; but the general effect of them
seemed to me so sad and so beautiful that I was thrilled

---

[1] Anatole France in *Livre de mon ami*, p. 118.

by a feeling that I had never known before—the charm of melancholy was revealed to me by a score of verses the literal meaning of which I could not have explained. The fact is that unless one has grown old, one does not need to understand deeply in order to feel deeply : things dimly comprehended can be quite touching, and it is very true that what is vague and indefinite has a charm for youth.'

There should be nothing, then, in this book which a lover of poetry will ever cast aside, and within its proper limitations the collection should be as gratifying to the old as to the young.

The motives of selection can be thus sufficiently stated, but the principles guiding exclusion are not so readily described. The conspicuous absence of several famous poets will be easily understood, although their disqualifications are very unlike in kind ; but the peculiar limitations of a book to be used in class may not be so well recognised, and they must be allowed for. On the other hand, it will be evident that some of the poems are too advanced for general use ; but here it has to be considered that in all schools there are exceptionally poetic pupils, and this book would fail in its aim if it neglected them. Nor is it improbable that these very poems will make the first appeal to minds that seem least impressionable.

One of the advantages for us of our classical education has been that the boys who learned Greek and Latin had only masterpieces to study : and if our cultured class have generally a surer and better taste in Greek or Latin poetry than they have in English, this may be attributed to the advantage they have had in the one and not in the other. The most of them, if asked their opinion on the merits of some favourite English poem, will tell you that on account of early association they are incapable of judging it, and in this predicament

even high intellect is found helpless ; the childish senti-
ment has become part of themselves, and with great
detriment to themselves, because reverence for a bad
model induces a liking for things of the same sort. Now
this association, which is so strong for inferior things, is
equally strong for the best ; and though an early attach-
ment may but seldom develop into adult judgment, yet
in the absence of that rare mature aesthetic appreciation
it is the best substitute for it.

And no one surely would deem it an accident that the
nation whose language was the most prevalent through-
out the world should be the nation which had the best
living poetry : an honour which we can assume without
prejudice, and value it not more as a badge of youthful
prowess than a lively means of continuous health and
advancement. And only by loving familiarity with it
can we securely guard our expanding and wandering
speech from all that sort of outward contamination and
indiscriminate mutation whereby its old nobility might
easily become estranged from the understanding of our
descendants—lest Shakespeare should ever be to them as
Homer is to the modern Greeks, more of a pitiful boast
than a living glory : and it has been both a credit and
profit to us that our nineteenth-century poets stood so
high in the scale of excellence, and preserved so well the
accent of our older poetry, that there is no gap in the
train of song, and to-day (except where our gentler
manners are offended) no word of Shakespeare need be
changed when his plays are acted to a London audience.

In this guardianship of our speech we shall find our
best security by enforcing and maintaining a high
standard of English in our school-books, which should
be the same for all classes : since the changes that
must come in our language will be made by the common
practice of the folk, who, if they are unfamiliar with
sound tradition, will develop usages out of all relation to

it and, indulging in the spontaneous accidental fashions of their unrelated environments, must break up into a hundred divergent dialects mutually unintelligible.

Dialects have always existed, and always will exist, and they should be fostered in their several habitats—their separate existence as living forces of original character is not incompatible with the preservation of the purity of the main stock, nor with that sense of touch with it which would keep them from eccentricities and distortion. Now if these two desirable things are to be assured, a schooling for all in the main or mother dialect is imperative.

And yet it has seemed to me that a lamentable disruption of our speech, which would eventually rob the British race of their noblest inheritance, might reasonably be predicted as its natural catastrophe beyond the scope of any prevision to remedy or avert, were it not for the recent astonishing inventions of Science, whereby the spoken word can be transmitted all over the world. Every man will wish to hear and understand the best speakers ; and all that we most needed and desired seems promised to us in the simplest solution of that problem, namely, that all, whatever dialect they speak at home, should hear the language of our great literature in wireless broadcasting, and through their normal schooling be familiar with it.

May our democracies have intelligence to make a right use of God's good gifts, and not leave this paramount and imperial means of national culture to be squandered in the selfish interests of commercialism !

CONTENTS

I love to rise in a summer morn
When the birds sing on every tree;
The distant huntsman winds his horn
And the skylark sings with me.
O! what sweet company.

THE CHILSWELL BOOK
OF ENGLISH POETRY

1   *Hunting Song*

WAKEN, lords and ladies gay,
On the mountain dawns the day ;
All the jolly chase is here,
With hawk and horse and hunting-spear :
Hounds are in their couples yelling,
Hawks are whistling, horns are knelling,
Merrily merrily mingle they ;
' Waken, lords and ladies gay.'

Waken, lords and ladies gay,
The mist has left the mountain gray,
Springlets in the dawn are streaming,
Diamonds on the brake are gleaming ;
And foresters have busy been
To track the buck in thicket green ;
Now we come to chant our lay,
' Waken, lords and ladies gay.'

Waken, lords and ladies gay,
To the greenwood haste away ;
We can show you where he lies,
Fleet of foot and tall of size ;
We can show the marks he made
When 'gainst the oak his antlers fray'd ;
You shall see him brought to bay ;
' Waken, lords and ladies gay '

A

Louder, louder chant the lay,
Waken, lords and ladies gay !
Tell them, youth and mirth and glee
Run a course as well as we ;
Time, stern huntsman ! who can baulk,
Staunch as hound and fleet as hawk ?
Think of this, and rise with day,
Gentle lords and ladies gay !

Scott.

2* ## Song from Cymbeline

Hark, hark ! the lark at heaven's gate sings,
  And Phœbus 'gins arise,
His steeds to water at those springs
  On chaliced flowers that lies ;
And winking Mary-buds begin
  To ope their golden eyes ;
With every thing that pretty is,
  My lady sweet, arise ;
    Arise, arise !

Shakespeare.

3 ## Song on May Morning

Now the bright morning Star, Day's harbinger,
Comes dancing from the East, and leads with her
The Flowery May, who from her green lap throws
The yellow Cowslip and the pale Primrose.
  Hail, bounteous May, that dost inspire
  Mirth and youth and warm desire ;
  Woods and Groves are of thy dressing,
  Hill and Dale doth boast thy blessing.
Thus we salute thee with our early Song,
And welcome thee, and wish thee long.

Milton.

harbinger] herald.

4   *The Echoing Green*

THE Sun does arise
And make happy the skies ;
The merry bells ring
To welcome the Spring ;
The skylark and thrush,
The birds of the bush,
Sing louder around
To the bells' cheerful sound ;
While our sports shall be seen
On the echoing Green.

Old John, with white hair,
Does laugh away care,
Sitting under the oak,
Among the old folk.
They laugh at our play,
And soon they all say,
' Such, such were the joys
When we all—girls and boys—
In our youth-time were seen
On the echoing Green.'

Till the little ones, weary,
No more can be merry ;
The sun does descend,
And our sports have an end.
Round the laps of their mothers
Many sisters and brothers,
Like birds in their nest,
Are ready for rest,
And sport no more seen
On the darkening Green.

Blake.

5

Under the greenwood tree
Who loves to lie with me,
And tune his merry note
Unto the sweet bird's throat—
Come hither, come hither, come hither !
    Here shall he see
    No enemy
But winter and rough weather.

Who doth ambition shun
And loves to live i' the sun,
Seeking the food he eats
And pleased with what he gets—
Come hither, come hither, come hither !
    Here shall he see
    No enemy
But winter and rough weather.

Shakespeare.

6

Orpheus with his lute made trees
And the mountain tops that freeze
   Bow themselves when he did sing :
To his music plants and flowers
Ever sprung ; as sun and showers
   There had made a lasting Spring.

Every thing that heard him play,
Even the billows of the sea,
   Hung their heads and then lay by.
In sweet music is such art,
Killing care and grief of heart
   Fall asleep, or hearing die.

Shakespeare.

7 *Spring*

SPRING, the sweet Spring, is the year's pleasant king;
Then blooms each thing, then maids dance in a ring,
Cold doth not sting, the pretty birds do sing,
    Cuckoo, jug-jug, pu-we, to-witta-woo !

The palm and may make country houses gay,
Lambs frisk and play, the shepherds pipe all day,
And we hear aye birds tune this merry lay,
    Cuckoo, jug-jug, pu-we, to-witta-woo !

The fields breathe sweet, the daisies kiss our feet,
Young lovers meet, old wives a-sunning sit,
In every street these tunes our ears do greet,
    Cuckoo, jug-jug, pu-we, to-witta-woo !
      Spring ! the sweet Spring !
                  Nashe.

8   *Ariel's Song*

    COME unto these yellow sands,
      And then take hands :
    Courtsied when you have and kiss'd
      The wild waves whist :
    Foot it featly here and there ;
    And, sweet sprites, the burden bear.
      Hark, hark !
BURDEN (*dispersedly*). Bowgh, waugh,
ARIEL.   The watch-dogs bark :
BURDEN (*dispersedly*). Bowgh, waugh.
ARIEL.   Hark, hark ! I hear
    The strain of strutting chanticleer
    Cry, Cock-a-diddle-dow !
              Shakespeare.
  whist] hushed.   burden] refrain.

9   *Fairy Song*

WHERE the bee sucks, there suck I :
In a cowslip's bell I lie ;
There I couch when owls do cry.
On the bat's back I do fly
After summer merrily.
Merrily, merrily shall I live now
Under the blossom that hangs on the bough.

         Shakespeare.

10   *Puck's Song*

Over hill, over dale,
 Thorough bush, thorough brier,
Over park, over pale,
 Thorough flood, thorough fire,
I do wander everywhere,
Swifter than the moonës sphere ;
And I serve the fairy queen,
To dew her orbs upon the green.
The cowslips tall her pensioners be ;
In their gold coats spots you see ;
Those be rubies, fairy favours,
In those freckles live their savours :
I must go seek some dew-drops here,
And hang a pearl in every cowslip's ear.

         Shakespeare.

11   *Meg Merrilies*

I

OLD Meg she was a Gipsy,
 And lived upon the moors :
Her bed it was the brown heath turf,
 And her house was out of doors.

thorough] through.   dew her orbs] bedew the fairy rings.

II

Her apples were swart blackberries,
　　Her currants pods o' broom ;
Her wine was dew of the wild white rose,
　　Her book a churchyard tomb.

III

Her Brothers were the craggy hills,
　　Her Sisters larchen trees—
Alone with her great family
　　She lived as she did please.

IV

No breakfast had she many a morn,
　　No dinner many a noon,
And 'stead of supper she would stare
　　Full hard against the Moon.

V

But every morn of Woodbine fresh
　　She made her garlanding,
And every night the dark glen Yew
　　She wove, and she would sing.

VI

And with her fingers old and brown
　　She plaited Mats o' Rushes,
And gave them to the Cottagers
　　She met among the Bushes.

VII

Old Meg was brave as Margaret Queen
　　And tall as Amazon :
An old red blanket cloak she wore ;
　　A chip hat had she on.
God rest her aged bones somewhere—
　　She died full long agone !

　　　　　　　　　　　　Keats.

12   *Weathers*

I

THIS is the weather the cuckoo likes,
    And so do I ;
When showers betumble the chestnut spikes,
    And nestlings fly :
And the little brown nightingale bills his best,
And they sit outside at ' The Travellers' Rest,'
And maids come forth sprig-muslin drest,
And citizens dream of the south and west,
    And so do I.

II

This is the weather the shepherd shuns,
    And so do I ;
When beeches drip in browns and duns,
    And thresh, and ply ;
The hill-hid tides throb, throe on throe,
And meadow rivulets overflow,
And drops on gate-bars hang in a row,
And rooks in families homeward go,
    And so do I.

                              Thomas Hardy.

13   *Winter*

WHEN icicles hang by the wall,
    And Dick the shepherd blows his nail,
And Tom bears logs into the hall,
    And milk comes frozen home in pail,
When blood is nipp'd, and ways be foul,
Then nightly sings the staring owl,
        To-whit !
To-who !—a merry note,
While greasy Joan doth keel the pot.

thresh and ply] toss and bend.
keel] cool, by stirring or adding something to prevent boiling over.

When all aloud the wind doth blow,
   And coughing drowns the parson's saw,
And birds sit brooding in the snow,
   And Marian's nose looks red and raw,
When roasted crabs hiss in the bowl,
Then nightly sings the staring owl,
     To-whit !
To-who !—a merry note,
While greasy Joan doth keel the pot.

Shakespeare.

14 *Answer to a Child's Question*

Do you ask what the birds say ?   The sparrow, the dove,
The linnet and thrush say, ' I love and I love ! '
In the winter they 're silent—the wind is so strong—
What it says I don't know, but it sings a loud song.
But green leaves, and blossoms, and sunny warm
    weather,
And singing, and loving, all come back together.
But the lark is so brimful of gladness and love,
The green fields below him, the blue sky above,
That he sings, and he sings, and for ever sings he—
' I love my Love, and my Love loves me ! '

Coleridge.

15 *Ophelia's Song*

How should I your true love know
   From another one ?
By his cockle hat and staff
   And his sandal shoon.

saw] sermon.   crabs] crab-apples.
cockle hat] hat with a cockle or scallop-shell stuck in it, as sign
that the wearer had visited the saint's shrine in Spain.

He is dead and gone, lady,
    He is dead and gone ;
At his head a grass-green turf,
    At his heels a stone.

White his shroud as the mountain snow,
    Larded with sweet flowers,
Which bewept to the grave did go
    With true-love showers.

                    Shakespeare.

16

Jog on, jog on, the footpath way,
    And merrily hent the stile-a :
A merry heart goes all the day,
    Your sad tires in a mile-a.

                    Shakespeare.

17

My heart 's in the Highlands, my heart is not here ;
My heart 's in the Highlands a-chasing the deer ;
Chasing the wild deer, and following the roe,
My heart 's in the Highlands, wherever I go.
Farewell to the Highlands, farewell to the North,
The birth-place of valour, the country of worth ;
Wherever I wander, wherever I rove,
The hills of the Highlands for ever I love.

Farewell to the mountains high cover'd with snow ;
Farewell to the straths and green valleys below ;
Farewell to the forests and wild-hanging woods ;
Farewell to the torrents and loud-pouring floods.

larded] stuck all over with.   hent] seize, lay hand on.
straths] low alluvial land, waterside meadows.

My heart 's in the Highlands, my heart is not here ;
My heart 's in the Highlands a-chasing the deer ;
Chasing the wild deer, and following the roe,
My heart 's in the Highlands, wherever I go.

Burns.

18   *The Vagabond*

GIVE to me the life I love,
  Let the lave go by me,
Give the jolly heaven above
  And the by-way nigh me.
Bed in the bush with stars to see,
  Bread I dip in the river—
There 's the life for a man like me,
  There 's the life for ever.

Let the blow fall soon or late,
  Let what will be o'er me ;
Give the face of earth around
  And the road before me.
Wealth I seek not, hope nor love,
  Nor a friend to know me ;
All I seek, the heaven above
  And the road below me.

Or let autumn fall on me
  Where afield I linger,
Silencing the bird on tree,
  Biting the blue finger.
White as meal the frosty field—
  Warm the fireside haven—
Not to autumn will I yield,
  Not to winter even !

          lave] remainder.

Let the blow fall soon or late,
　　Let what will be o'er me ;
Give the face of earth around,
　　And the road before me.
Wealth I ask not, hope nor love,
　　Nor a friend to know me.
All I ask, the heaven above,
　　And the road below me.

Stevenson.

19　　*On the Hearth-Rug*

' LITTLE tongue of red-brown flame,
Whither go you ? '—' Whence I came ;
Sending on a courier spark
To explore the chimney dark.

' Once I was a sunbeam fair,
Darting thro' the awaken'd air.
Quickly to a green leaf gone,
On a forest tree I shone.

' Steely lightning struck the bough,
And I sank into a slough.
Many ages there I lay,
Ere I saw the All-Father, Day.

' Now I sparkle once again,
Flashing light and warmth to men,
Ere, like all things that are bright,
I rejoin the All-Mother, Night.'

Mary Coleridge.

20

> If thou wast still, O stream,
> Thou would'st be frozen now :
> And 'neath an icy shield
> Thy current warm would flow.
>
> But wild thou art and rough ;
> And so the bitter breeze,
> That chafes thy shuddering waves,
> May never bid thee freeze.
>
> *Dixon.*

21   *The Minstrel-Boy*

> The Minstrel-boy to the war is gone,
> In the ranks of death you 'll find him ;
> His father's sword he has girded on,
> And his wild harp slung behind him.—
> ' Land of song ! ' said the warrior-bard,
> ' Though all the world betrays thee,
> *One* sword, at least, thy rights shall guard,
> *One* faithful harp shall praise thee ! '
>
> The Minstrel fell !—but the foeman's chain
> Could not bring his proud soul under ;
> The harp he loved ne'er spoke again,
> For he tore its chords asunder ;
> And said, ' No chains shall sully thee,
> Thou soul of love and bravery !
> Thy songs were made for the brave and free :
> They shall never sound in slavery ! '
>
> *Moore.*

22   *Ye Mariners of England*

Ye mariners of England,
   That guard our native seas !
Whose flag has braved a thousand years
   The battle and the breeze !
Your glorious standard launch again
   To match another foe !
         And sweep through the deep,
         While the stormy winds do blow ;
         While the battle rages loud and long,
         And the stormy winds do blow.

The spirits of your fathers
   Shall start from every wave—
For the deck it was their field of fame,
   And Ocean was their grave :
Where Blake and mighty Nelson fell
   Your manly hearts shall glow,
         As ye sweep through the deep,
         While the stormy winds do blow ;
         While the battle rages loud and long,
         And the stormy winds do blow.

Britannia needs no bulwarks,
   No towers along the steep ;
Her march is o'er the mountain waves,
   Her home is on the deep.
With thunders from her native oak
   She quells the floods below—
         As they roar on the shore,
         When the stormy winds do blow ;
         When the battle rages loud and long,
         And the stormy winds do blow.

The meteor flag of England
  Shall yet terrific burn ;
Till danger's troubled night depart,
  And the star of peace return.
Then, then, ye ocean-warriors !
  Our song and feast shall flow
      To the fame of your name,
    When the storm hath ceased to blow ;
    When the fiery fight is heard no more,
    And the storm has ceased to blow.

Campbell

23　　　　　*Ellen's Song*

SOLDIER, rest ! thy warfare o'er,
  Sleep the sleep that knows not breaking ;
Dream of battled fields no more,
  Days of danger, nights of waking.
In our isle's enchanted hall,
  Hands unseen thy couch are strewing,
Fairy strains of music fall,
  Every sense in slumber dewing.
Soldier, rest ! thy warfare o'er,
Dream of fighting fields no more :
Sleep the sleep that knows not breaking,
Morn of toil, nor night of waking.

No rude sound shall reach thine ear,
  Armour's clang, or war-steed champing ;
Trump nor pibroch summon here
  Mustering clan, or squadron tramping.

meteor flag] flashing like a meteor.
dewing] steeping, immersing.
pibroch] a martial air or dirge on bagpipe : *pi* pronounced as *pea*.

Yet the lark's shrill fife may come
  At the daybreak from the fallow,
And the bittern sound his drum,
  Booming from the sedgy shallow.
Ruder sounds shall none be near,
Guards nor warders challenge here,
Here's no war-steed's neigh and champing,
Shouting clans, or squadrons stamping. . . .

Scott.

24 The Burial of Sir John Moore

NOT a drum was heard, not a funeral note,
  As his corpse to the rampart we hurried ;
Not a soldier discharged his farewell shot
  O'er the grave where our hero we buried.

We buried him darkly at dead of night,
  The sods with our bayonets turning,
By the struggling moonbeam's misty light,
  And the lantern dimly burning.

No useless coffin enclosed his breast,
  Not in sheet or in shroud we wound him ;
But he lay like a warrior taking his rest,
  With his martial cloak around him.

Few and short were the prayers we said,
  And we spoke not a word of sorrow,
But we steadfastly gazed on the face that was dead,
  And we bitterly thought of the morrow :

We thought, as we hollow'd his narrow bed
  And smooth'd down his lonely pillow,
That the foe and the stranger would tread o'er his head,
  And we far away on the billow !

Lightly they 'll talk of the spirit that 's gone,
    And o'er his cold ashes upbraid him ;
But little he 'll reck, if they let him sleep on
    In the grave where a Briton has laid him.

But half of our heavy task was done,
    When the clock struck the hour for retiring :
And we heard the distant and random gun
    That the foe was sullenly firing.

Slowly and sadly we laid him down,
    From the field of his fame fresh and gory :
We carved not a line, we raised not a stone,
    But we left him alone with his glory.

                                    Wolfe.

25 The Loss of the 'Royal George'

TOLL for the brave !
    The brave that are no more !
All sunk beneath the wave
    Fast by their native shore !

Eight hundred of the brave,
    Whose courage well was tried,
Had made the vessel heel,
    And laid her on her side.

A land-breeze shook the shrouds,
    And she was overset ;
Down went the *Royal George*,
    With all her crew complete.

Toll for the brave !
    Brave Kempenfelt is gone ;
His last sea-fight is fought,
    His work of glory done.

B

It was not in the battle ;
   No tempest gave the shock ;
She sprang no fatal leak ;
   She ran upon no rock.

His sword was in its sheath,
   His fingers held the pen,
When Kempenfelt went down
   With twice four hundred men.

Weigh the vessel up
   Once dreaded by our foes !
And mingle with our cup
   The tear that England owes

Her timbers yet are sound,
   And she may float again
Full charged with England's thunder,
   And plough the distant main.

But Kempenfelt is gone,
   His victories are o'er ;
And he and his eight hundred
   Shall plough the wave no more.

                    Cowper.

26   *To Abraham Lincoln*

O CAPTAIN ! my Captain ! our fearful trip is done,
The ship has weather'd every rack, the prize we sought
    is won,
The port is near, the bells I hear, the people all exulting,
While follow eyes the steady keel, the vessel grim and
    daring ;
        But O heart ! heart ! heart !
          O the bleeding drops of red !
            Where on the deck my Captain lies,
              Fallen cold and dead.

O Captain ! my Captain ! rise up and hear the bells ;
Rise up—for you the flag is flung—for you the bugle
    trills,
For you bouquets and ribbon'd wreaths—for you the
    shores a-crowding,
For you they call, the swaying mass, their eager faces
    turning ;
        Here, Captain ! dear father !
          This arm beneath your head !
            It is some dream that on the deck
              You 've fallen cold and dead.

My Captain does not answer, his lips are pale and still,
My father does not feel my arm, he has no pulse nor will ;
The ship is anchor'd safe and sound, its voyage closed
    and done,
From fearful trip the victor ship comes in with object
    won ;
        Exult, O shores ! and ring, O bells !
        But I, with mournful tread,
          Walk the deck my Captain lies'
          Fallen cold and dead.

                        Whitman.

27   *Dirge*

    How sleep the Brave, who sink to rest
    By all their Country's wishes blest !
    When Spring, with dewy fingers cold,
    Returns to deck their hallow'd mould,
    She there shall dress a sweeter sod
    Than Fancy's feet have ever trod.

    By fairy hands their knell is rung ;
    By forms unseen their dirge is sung ;

There Honour comes, a pilgrim grey,
To bless the turf that wraps their clay ;
And Freedom shall awhile repair
To dwell a weeping hermit there !

Collins, 1746.

28

WHERE shall the lover rest
   Whom the fates sever
From his true maiden's breast,
   Parted for ever ?
Where through groves deep and high
   Sounds the far billow,
Where early violets die
   Under the willow :—
     Eleu loro !
     Soft shall be his pillow.

There, through the summer day,
   Cool streams are laving ;
There, while the tempests sway,
   Scarce are boughs waving ;
There thy rest shalt thou take,
   Parted for ever,
Never again to wake,
   Never, O never !
     Eleu loro !
     Never, O never !

Where shall the traitor rest,
   He, the deceiver,
Who could win maiden's breast,
   Ruin, and leave her ?

In the lost battle,
    Borne down by the flying,
Where mingles war's rattle
    With groans of the dying.
        Eleu loro !
        There shall he be lying.

Her wing shall the eagle flap
    O'er the false-hearted ;
His warm blood the wolf shall lap,
    Ere life be parted ;
Shame and dishonour sit
    By his grave ever ;
Blessing shall hallow it,—
    Never, O never !
        Eleu loro !
        Never, O never !

                                        Scott.

29   *Ariel Sings*

FULL fathom five thy father lies :
    Of his bones are coral made ;
Those are pearls that were his eyes :
    Nothing of him that doth fade,
    But doth suffer a sea-change
    Into something rich and strange.
    Sea-nymphs hourly ring his knell :
BURDEN.   *Ding-dong.*
    Hark ! now I hear them,—ding-dong, bell.
                            Shakespeare.

30   *Requiem*

UNDER the wide and starry sky
Dig the grave and let me lie.
Glad did I live and gladly die,
    And I laid me down with a will.

burden] refrain heard sung by the sea-nymphs.

This be the verse you grave for me :
Here he lies where he longed to be ;
Home is the sailor, home from the sea,
And the hunter home from the hill.

Stevenson, 1884.

Song

31

STAY, stay at home, my heart, and rest ;
Home-keeping hearts are happiest,
For those that wander they know not where
Are full of trouble and full of care ;
To stay at home is best.

Weary and homesick and distress'd,
They wander east, they wander west,
And are baffled and beaten and blown about
By the winds of the wilderness of doubt ;
To stay at home is best.

Then stay at home, my heart, and rest ;
The bird is safest in its nest ;
O'er all that flutter their wings and fly
A hawk is hovering in the sky ;
To stay at home is best.

Longfellow.

Lucy Ashton's Song

32

LOOK not thou on beauty's charming ;
Sit thou still when kings are arming ;
Taste not when the wine-cup glistens ;
Speak not when the people listens ;
Stop thine ear against the singer ;
From the red gold keep thy finger ;
Vacant heart and hand and eye,
Easy live and quiet die.

Scott.

33 *Nurse's Song*

WHEN the voices of children are heard on the green,
    And laughing is heard on the hill,
My heart is at rest within my breast,
    And everything else is still.

' Then come home, my children, the sun is gone down,
    And the dews of night arise ;
Come, come, leave off play, and let us away
    Till the morning appears in the skies.'

' No, no, let us play, for it is yet day,
    And we cannot go to sleep ;
Besides, in the sky the little birds fly,
    And the hills are all cover'd with sheep.'

' Well, well, go and play till the light fades away,
    And then go home to bed.'
The little ones leapèd and shouted and laugh'd
    And all the hills echoèd.

Blake.

34* *Night*

THE sun descending in the west,
    The evening star does shine ;
The birds are silent in their nest,
    And I must seek for mine.
The moon, like a flower,
In heaven's high bower,
With silent delight
Sits and smiles on the night.

Farewell, green fields and happy groves,
    Where flocks have took delight.
Where lambs have nibbled, silent moves
    The feet of angels bright ;

took] common in dialect and vulgar speech for *taken.*
moves] see note at end of book.

Unseen they pour blessing,
And joy without ceasing,
On each bud and blossom,
And each sleeping bosom.

They look in every thoughtless nest,
    Where birds are cover'd warm ;
They visit caves of every beast,
    To keep them all from harm.
If they see any weeping
That should have been sleeping,
They pour sleep on their head,
And sit down by their bed. . . .

Blake.

35   *Cradle Song*

Sweet and low, sweet and low,
    Wind of the western sea,
Low, low, breathe and blow,
    Wind of the western sea !
Over the rolling waters go,
Come from the dying moon, and blow,
    Blow him again to me ;
While my little one, while my pretty one, sleeps.

Sleep and rest, sleep and rest,
    Father will come to thee soon ;
Rest, rest, on mother's breast,
    Father will come to thee soon ;
Father will come to his babe in the nest,
Silver sails all out of the west
    Under the silver moon :
Sleep, my little one, sleep, my pretty one, sleep.

Tennyson.

36   *Lullaby of an Infant Chief*

Oн ! hush thee, my babie, thy sire was a knight,
Thy mother a lady both lovely and bright :
The woods and the glens, from the towers which we see,
They all are belonging, dear babie, to thee.

Oh ! fear not the bugle, though loudly it blows,
It calls but the warders that guard thy repose ;
Their bows would be bended, their blades would be red,
Ere the step of a foeman draws near to thy bed.

Oh ! hush thee, my babie, the time soon will come,
When thy sleep shall be broken by trumpet and drum ;
Then hush thee, my darling, take rest while you may,
For strife comes with manhood, and waking with day.
Scott, 1815.

37   *A Faery Song*

(Sung by the Fairies over an outlaw and his bride
who had escaped into the mountains.)

We who are old, old and gay,
O so old !
Thousand of years, thousand of years,
If all were told :

Give to these children, new from the world,
Silence and love ;
And the long dew-dropping hours of the night,
And the stars above :

Give to these children, new from the world,
    Rest far from men.
Is anything better, anything better ?
    Tell us it then :

Us who are old, old and gay,
    O so old !
Thousand of years, thousand of years,
    If all were told.

W. B. Yeats.

38*

IT is not growing like a tree
In bulk, doth make men better be ;
Or standing long an oak, three hundred year,
To fall a log at last, dry, bald, and sere ;
    A lily of a day
    Is fairer far in May,
Although it fall and die that night ;
It was the plant and flower of Light.
In small proportions we just beauties see ;
And in short measures life may perfect be.

Ben Jonson.

39*   *Life*

. . . Joy and Woe are woven fine,
A Clothing for the soul divine :
Under every grief and pine
Runs a joy with silken twine.
It is right it should be so :
Man was made for Joy and Woe ;
And when this we rightly know,
Safely through the World we go. . . .

Blake.

40* *Hymn on the Morning of Christ's Nativity*

I

It was the Winter wild,
While the Heav'n-born-child
   All meanly wrapt in the rude manger lies ;
Nature in awe to him
Had doff'd her gaudy trim,
   With her great Master so to sympathize :
It was no season then for her
To wanton with the Sun her lusty Paramour.

II

Only with speeches fair
She woos the gentle Air
   To hide her guilty front with innocent Snow ;
And on her naked shame,
Pollute with sinful blame,
   The saintly Veil of maiden white to throw,
Confounded, that her Maker's eyes
Should look so near upon her foul deformities.

III

But he, her fears to cease,
Sent down the meek-eyed Peace ;
   She, crown'd with Olive green, came softly sliding
Down through the turning sphere
His ready Harbinger,
   With Turtle wing the amorous clouds dividing ;
And waving wide her myrtle wand,
She strikes a universal Peace through Sea and Land.

i. paramour] lover.   ii. front] forehead.
iii. **turning sphere]***.   harbinger] herald.   turtle] dove.

IV

No War, or Battle's sound
Was heard the World around,
   The idle spear and shield were high up-hung ;
The hookèd Chariot stood
Unstain'd with hostile blood,
   The Trumpet spake not to the armèd throng,
And Kings sat still with aweful eye,
As if they surely knew their sovran Lord was by.

V

But peaceful was the night
Wherein the Prince of light
   His reign of peace upon the earth began :
The Winds with wonder whist,
Smoothly the waters kiss'd,
   Whispering new joys to the mild Oceän,
Who now hath quite forgot to rave,
While Birds of Calm sit brooding on the charmèd wave.

VI

The Stars with deep amaze
Stand fix'd in stedfast gaze,
   Bending one way their precious influence,
And will not take their flight,
For all the morning light,
   Or *Lucifer* that often warn'd them thence ;
But in their glimmering Orbs did glow,
Until their Lord himself bespake, and bid them go.

VII

And though the shady gloom
Had given day her room,
   The Sun himself with-held his wonted speed,

<hr>

IV. hooked] with hooks on axles.   V. whist] hushed.

And hid his head for shame,
As his inferior flame
   The new enlightn'd world no more should need :
He saw a greater Sun appear
Than his bright Throne or burning Axletree could bear.

VIII

The Shepherds on the Lawn,
Or ere the point of dawn,
   Sat simply chatting in a rustic row ;
Full little thought they than,
That the mighty *Pan*
   Was kindly come to live with them below ;
Perhaps their loves, or else their sheep,
Was all that did their silly thoughts so busy keep.

IX

When such music sweet
Their hearts and ears did greet,
   As never was by mortal finger strook,
Divinely-warbled voice
Answering the stringèd noise,
   As all their souls in blissful rapture took :
The Air such pleasure loth to lose,
With thousand echoes still prolongs each heav'nly close.

X

Nature, that heard such sound
Beneath the hollow round
   Of *Cynthia's* seat, the Airy region thrilling,
Now was almost won
To think her part was done,
   And that her reign had here its last fulfilling ;
She knew such harmony alone
Could hold all Heav'n and Earth in happier uniòn,

VII. as] as if.   axle-tree] the fixed beam on which the wheels turn.
VIII. or ere] before.   than] old form of *then*.   silly] simple.
IX. close] cadence.   x. round, etc.]*.

XI

At last surrounds their sight
A Globe of circular light,
 That with long beams the shamefaced night array'd,
The helmèd Cherubim
And sworded Seraphim,
 Are seen in glittering ranks with wings display'd,
Harping in loud and solemn quire
With unexpressive notes to Heaven's new-born Heir.

XII

Such Music (as 'tis said)
Before was never made,
 But when of old the sons of morning sung,
While the Creator Great
His constellations set,
 And the well-balanced world on hinges hung ;
And cast the dark foundations deep,
And bid the weltering waves their oozy channel keep.

XIII

Ring out ye Crystal spheres !
Once bless our human ears,
 (If ye have power to touch our senses so)
And let your silver chime
Move in melodious time ;
 And let the Bass of Heav'n's deep Organ blow,
And with your ninefold harmony
Make up full consort to th' Angelic symphony.

XIV

For if such holy Song
Enwrap our fancy long,
 Time will run back, and fetch the age of gold ;

XI. unexpressive] inexpressible.
XIII. crystal spheres]*.   consort] orchestra, concert.

And speckled vanity
Will sicken soon and die,
   And leprous sin will melt from earthly mould ;
And Hell itself will pass away,
And leave her dolorous mansions to the peering day

XV

Yea, Truth and Justice then
Will down return to men,
   Orb'd in a Rain-bow ; and like glories wearing
Mercy will sit between,
Throned in Celestial sheen,
   With radiant feet the tissued clouds down steering,
And Heav'n, as at some festival,
Will open wide the Gates of her high Palace Hall.

XVI

But wisest Fate says No ;
This must not yet be so ;
   The Babe lies yet in smiling Infancy,
That on the bitter cross
Must redeem our loss ;
   So both himself and us to glorify :
Yet first to those ychain'd in sleep,
The wakeful trump of doom must thunder through the
    deep,

XVII

With such a horrid clang
As on mount *Sinai* rang
   While the red fire, and smouldering clouds outbrake :
The agèd Earth aghast
With terror of that blast,
   Shall from the surface to the centre shake,
When at the world's last sessiòn,
The dreadful Judge in middle Air shall spread his throne.

xiv. speckled] plague-spotted.   xvii. session] sitting in judgment.

XVIII

And then at last our bliss
Full and perfect is,
   But now begins ; for from this happy day
Th' old Dragon under ground
In straiter limits bound,
   Not half so far casts his usurpèd sway ;
And wroth to see his Kingdom fail,
Swindges the scaly Horror of his folded tail.

XIX

The Oracles are dumb ;
No voice or hideous hum
   Runs through the archèd roof in words deceiving.
Apollo from his shrine
Can no more divine,
   With hollow shriek the steep of *Delphos* leaving :
No nightly trance, or breathèd spell,
Inspires the pale-eyed Priest from the prophetic cell.

XX

The lonely mountains o'er,
And the resounding shore,
   A voice of weeping heard, and loud lament ;
From haunted spring, and dale,
Edged with poplar pale,
   The parting Genius is with sighing sent ;
With flower-inwoven tresses torn
The Nymphs in twilight shade of tangled thickets mourn.

XXI

In consecrated Earth
And on the holy Hearth
   The *Lars* and *Lemures* moan with midnight plaint,
In Urns, and Altars round,

xix. divine] give oracles.   xx. genius] spirit of the place.

A drear and dying sound
   Affrights the *Flamens* at their service quaint ;
And the chill marble seems to sweat,
While each peculiar power forgoes his wonted seat.

XXII

Peor and *Baalim*
Forsake their Temples dim,
   With that twice-batter'd god of *Palestine* ;
And moonèd *Ashtaroth*,
Heav'n's Queen and Mother both,
   Now sits not girt with tapers' holy shine ;
The Lybic *Hammon* shrinks his horn ;
In vain the *Tyrian* maids their wounded *Thammuz* mourn.

XXIII

And sullen *Moloch* fled,
Hath left in shadows dread
   His burning Idol all of blackest hue ;
In vain with cymbals' ring,
They call the grisly king,
   In dismal dance about the furnace blue ;
The brutish gods of *Nile* as fast,
Isis and *Orus*, and the Dog *Anubis* haste.

XXIV

Nor is *Osiris* seen
In *Memphian* Grove, or Green,
   Trampling the unshower'd grass with lowings loud :
Nor can he be at rest
Within his sacred chest ;
   Naught but profoundest Hell can be his shroud ;
In vain with Timbrel'd Anthems dark
The sable-stolèd Sorcerers bear his worshipt Ark.

XXIV. stoled] cloaked.
C

XXV

He feels from *Juda's* Land
The dreaded Infant's hand ;
  The rays of *Bethlehem* blind his dusky eyn ;
Nor all the gods beside,
Longer dare abide,
  Not *Typhon* huge ending in snaky twine :
Our Babe, to shew his Godhead true,
Can in his swaddling bands control the damnèd crew.

XXVI

So when the Sun in bed,
Curtain'd with cloudy red,
  Pillows his chin upon an Orient wave,
The flocking shadows pale,
Troop to th' infernal jail,
  Each fetter'd Ghost slips to his several grave ;
And the yellow-skirted *Fays*
Fly after the Night-steeds, leaving their Moon-lov'd
    maze.

XXVII

But see, the Virgin blest
Hath laid her Babe to rest ;
  Time is our tedious Song should here have ending ;
Heav'n's youngest-teemèd Star
Hath fix'd her polish'd Car,
  Her sleeping Lord with Handmaid Lamp attending :
And all about the courtly Stable,
Bright-harness'd Angels sit in order serviceable.

Milton, 1629.

XXVII. youngest-teemed] latest born, that is the star of Bethlehem.
fixed] stood still over the stable.   harnessed] armoured.

41* *Christmas Antiphon*

THOU whose birth on earth
   Angels sang to men,
While thy stars made mirth,
Saviour, at thy birth,
   This day born again ;

As this night was bright
   With thy cradle-ray,
Very light of light,
Turn the wild world's night
   To thy perfect day. . . .

Thou the Word and Lord
   In all time and space
Heard, beheld, adored,
With all ages pour'd
   Forth before thy face.

Lord, what worth in earth
   Drew thee down to die ?
What therein was worth,
Lord, thy death and birth ?
   What beneath thy sky ? . . .

From the height of night,
   Was not thine the star
That led forth with might
By no worldly light
   Wise men from afar ? . . .

Bid our peace increase,
   Thou that madest morn ;
Bid oppressions cease ;
Bid the night be peace ;
   Bid the day be born.

Swinburne.

42 *The New Jerusalem*

AND did those feet in ancient time
Walk upon England's mountains green ?
And was the holy Lamb of God
On England's pleasant pastures seen ?

And did the Countenance Divine
Shine forth upon our clouded hills ?
And was Jerusalem builded here
Among these dark Satanic mills ?

Bring me my Bow of burning gold !
Bring me my Arrows of desire !
Bring me my Spear !   O clouds, unfold !
Bring me my Chariot of fire !

I will not cease from Mental Fight,
Nor shall my Sword sleep in my hand,
Till we have built Jerusalem
In England's green and pleasant Land.

Blake.

43

ENGLAND ! awake ! awake ! awake !
Jerusalem thy Sister calls !
Why wilt thou sleep the sleep of death,
And close her from thy ancient walls ?

Thy hills and valleys felt her feet
Gently upon their bosoms move :
Thy Gates beheld sweet Zion's ways ;
Then was a time of joy and love.

And now the time returns again :
Our souls exult, and London's towers
Receive the Lamb of God to dwell
In England's green and pleasant bowers.

Blake.

44*   *Tiger*

TIGER ! tiger ! burning bright
In the forests of the night,
What immortal hand or eye
Could frame thy fearful symmetry ?

In what distant deeps or skies
Burnt the fire of thine eyes ?
On what wings dare he aspire ?
What the hand dare seize the fire ?

And what shoulder, and what art,
Could twist the sinews of thy heart ?
And when thy heart began to beat,
What dread hand, and what dread feet ?

What the hammer ? what the chain ?
In what furnace was thy brain ?
What the anvil ? what dread grasp
Dare its deadly terrors clasp ?

When the stars threw down their spears,
And water'd heaven with their tears,
Did he smile his work to see ?
Did he who made the Lamb make thee ?

Tiger ! tiger ! burning bright
In the forests of the night,
What immortal hand or eye
Dare frame thy fearful symmetry ?

Blake.

45   *The Eagle*

HE clasps the crag with crooked hands ;
Close to the sun in lonely lands,
Ring'd with the azure world, he stands.

The wrinkled sea beneath him crawls ;
He watches from his mountain walls,
And like a thunderbolt he falls.

Tennyson.

46   *Alexander Selkirk during his Solitary*
Abode in the Island of Juan Fer-
nandez

I AM monarch of all I survey ;
    My right there is none to dispute ;
From the centre all round to the sea
    I am lord of the fowl and the brute.
O Solitude ! where are the charms
    That sages have seen in thy face ?
Better dwell in the midst of alarms
    Than reign in this horrible place.

I am out of humanity's reach,
    I must finish my journey alone,
Never hear the sweet music of speech ;
    I start at the sound of my own.
The beasts that roam over the plain
    My form with indifference see ;
They are so unacquainted with man,
    Their tameness is shocking to me.

Society, Friendship, and Love,
  Divinely bestow'd upon man,
O had I the wings of a dove,
  How soon would I taste you again !
My sorrows I then might assuage
  In the ways of religion and truth,
Might learn from the wisdom of age,
  And be cheer'd by the sallies of youth.

.   .   .   .   .   .

Ye winds that have made me your sport,
  Convey to this desolate shore
Some cordial endearing report
  Of a land I shall visit no more !
My friends, do they now and then send
  A wish or a thought after me ?
O tell me I yet have a friend,
  Though a friend I am never to see.

How fleet is a glance of the mind !
  Compared with the speed of its flight,
The tempest itself lags behind,
  And the swift wingèd arrows of light.
When I think of my own native land,
  In a moment I seem to be there ;
But alas ! recollection at hand
  Soon hurries me back to despair.

But the sea-fowl has gone to her nest,
  The beast is laid down in his lair ;
Even here is a season of rest,
  And I to my cabin repair.
There 's mercy in every place ;
  And mercy, encouraging thought !
Gives even affliction a grace,
  And reconciles man to his lot.

Cowper.

47   *The Banished Duke living in the Fores*
speaks to his Retainers

From *As You Like It*, II.

Now, my co-mates, and brothers in exile,
Hath not old custom made this life more sweet
Than that of painted pomp ?   Are not these woods
More free from peril than the envious court ?
Here feel we but the penalty of Adam,
The seasons' difference ;—as the icy fang
And churlish chiding of the winter's wind,
Which, when it bites and blows upon my body,
Even till I shrink with cold, I smile, and say
' This is no flattery ;—these are counsellors
That feelingly persuade me what I am.'—
Sweet are the uses of adversity ;
Which, like the toad, ugly and venemous,
Wears yet a precious jewel in his head :
And this our life exempt from public haunt
Finds tongues in trees, books in the running brooks
Sermons in stones and good in everything.
I would not change it.
    AMIENS.   Happy is your Grace,
That can translate the stubbornness of fortune
Into so quiet and so sweet a style. . . .
                              Shakespeare.

48*   *The Ancient Mariner*

PART I

IT is an ancient Mariner,
And he stoppeth one of three.
—' By thy long gray beard and glittering eye,
Now wherefore stopp'st thou me ?

    a precious jewel] refers to an old popular belief.

' The Bridegroom's doors are open'd wide,
And I am next of kin ;
The guests are met, the feast is set :
May'st hear the merry din.'

He holds him with his skinny hand,
  There was a ship,' quoth he.
—' Hold off ! unhand me, gray-beard loon ! '
Eftsoons his hand dropt he.

He holds him with his glittering eye :—
The Wedding-Guest stood still,
And listens like a three years' child :
The Mariner hath his will.

The Wedding-Guest sat on a stone :
He cannot choose but hear ;
And thus spake on that ancient man,
The bright-eyed Mariner :—

' The ship was cheer'd, the harbour clear'd ;
Merrily did we drop
Below the kirk, below the hill,
Below the light-house top.

' The Sun came up upon the left,
Out of the sea came he !
And he shone bright, and on the right
Went down into the sea.

' Higher and higher every day,
Till over the mast at noon '—
The Wedding-Guest here beat his breast,
For he heard the loud bassoon.

eftsoons] at once.

The bride hath paced into the hall,
Red as a rose is she ;
Nodding their heads before her goes
The merry minstrelsy.

The Wedding-Guest he beat his breast,
Yet he cannot choose but hear ;
And thus spake on that ancient man,
The bright-eyed Mariner :—

' And now the storm-blast came, and he
Was tyrannous and strong :
He struck with his o'ertaking wings,
And chased us south along.

' With sloping masts and dipping prow,
As who pursued with yell and blow
Still treads the shadow of his foe,
And forward bends his head,
The ship drove fast, loud roar'd the blast,
And southward aye we fled.

' And now there came both mist and snow,
And it grew wondrous cold :
And ice, mast-high, came floating by,
As green as emerald.

' And through the drifts the snowy clifts
Did send a dismal sheen :
Nor shapes of men nor beasts we ken—
The ice was all between.

' The ice was here, the ice was there,
The ice was all around :
It crack'd and growl'd, and roar'd and howl'd,
Like noises in a swound !

minstrelsy] musicians.   sheen] subst., shining.   swound] swoon

' At length did cross an Albatross,
Thorough the fog it came ;
As if it had been a Christian soul,
We hail'd it in God's name.

' It ate the food it ne'er had eat,
And round and round it flew.
The ice did split with a thunder-fit ;
The helmsman steer'd us through !

' And a good south wind sprung up behind ;
The Albatross did follow,
And every day, for food or play,
Came to the mariners' hollo !

' In mist or cloud, on mast or shroud,
It perch'd for vespers nine ;
Whiles all the night, through fog-smoke white,
Glimmer'd the white moon-shine.'

' God save thee, ancient Mariner !
From the fiends, that plague thee thus !—
Why look'st thou so ? '—' With my cross-bow
I shot the Albatross.

Part II

' The Sun now rose upon the right :
Out of the sea came he,
Still hid in mist,—and on the left
Went down into the sea.

' And the good south wind still blew behind,
But no sweet bird did follow,
Nor any day for food or play
Came to the mariners' hollo !

Albatross] great sea-bird.
the food it ne'er had eat] biscuit-worms.   shroud] rigging.

' And I had done a hellish thing,
And it would work 'em woe :
For all averr'd, I had kill'd the bird
That made the breeze to blow.
Ah wretch ! said they, the bird to slay,
That made the breeze to blow !

' Nor dim nor red, like God's own head,
The glorious Sun uprist :
Then all averr'd, I had kill'd the bird
That brought the fog and mist.
'Twas right, said they, such birds to slay,
That bring the fog and mist.

' The fair breeze blew, the white foam flew,
The furrow stream'd off free ;
We were the first that ever burst
Into that silent sea.

' Down dropt the breeze, the sails dropt down,
'Twas sad as sad could be ;
And we did speak only to break
The silence of the sea !

' All in a hot and copper sky,
The bloody Sun, at noon,
Right up above the mast did stand,
No bigger than the Moon.

' Day after day, day after day,
We stuck, nor breath nor motion ;
As idle as a painted ship
Upon a painted ocean.

' Water, water, everywhere,
And all the boards did shrink ;
Water, water, everywhere,
Nor any drop to drink.

'The very deep did rot : O Christ !
That ever this should be !
Yea, slimy things did crawl with legs
Upon the slimy sea.

' About, about, in reel and rout
The death-fires danced at night ;
The water, like a witch's oils,
Burnt green and blue and white.

' And some in dreams assurèd were
Of the Spirit that plagued us so ;
Nine fathom deep he had follow'd us
From the Land of Mist and Snow.

' And every tongue, through utter drought,
Was wither'd at the root ;
We could not speak, no more than if
We had been choked with soot.

' Ah ! well a-day ! what evil looks
Had I from old and young !
Instead of the cross, the Albatross
About my neck was hung.

Part III

' There pass'd a weary time.   Each throat
Was parch'd, and glazed each eye.
A weary time ! a weary time !
How glazed each weary eye !
When looking westward, I beheld
A something in the sky.

' At first it seem'd a little speck,
And then it seem'd a mist ;
It moved and moved, and took at last
A certain shape, I wist.

wist] perceived.

A speck, a mist, a shape, I wist !
And still it near'd and near'd :
As if it dodged a water-sprite,
It plunged and tack'd and veer'd.

' With throats unslaked, with black lips baked,
We could not laugh nor wail ;
Through utter drought all dumb we stood !
I bit my arm, I suck'd the blood,
And cried, A sail ! a sail !

' With throats unslaked, with black lips baked,
Agape they heard me call :
Gramercy ! they for joy did grin,
And all at once their breath drew in,
As they were drinking all.

' See ! see ! (I cried) she tacks no more !
Hither to work us weal ;
Without a breeze, without a tide,
She steadies with upright keel !

' The western wave was all a-flame,
The day was wellnigh done !
Almost upon the western wave
Rested the broad bright Sun ;
When that strange shape drove suddenly
Betwixt us and the Sun.

' And straight the Sun was fleck'd with bars,
(Heaven's Mother send us grace !)
As if through a dungeon-grate he peer'd
With broad and burning face.

' Alas ! (thought I, and my heart beat loud)
How fast she nears and nears !
Are those her sails that glance in the Sun,
Like restless gossameres ?

' Are those her ribs through which the Sun
Did peer, as through a grate ?
And is that Woman all her crew ?
Is that a Death ? and are there two ?
Is Death that Woman's mate ?

' Her lips were red, her looks were free,
Her locks were yellow as gold :
Her skin was as white as leprosy,
The Nightmare Life-in-Death was she,
Who thicks man's blood with cold.

' The naked hulk alongside came,
And the twain were casting dice ;
" The game is done ! I 've won ! I 've won ! "
Quoth she, and whistles thrice.

' The Sun's rim dips ; the stars rush out :
At one stride comes the dark ;
With far-heard whisper, o'er the sea,
Off shot the spectre-bark.

' We listen'd and look'd sideways up !
Fear at my heart, as at a cup,
My life-blood seem'd to sip !
The stars were dim, and thick the night,
The steersman's face by his lamp gleam'd white ;
From the sails the dew did drip—
Till clomb above the eastern bar
The hornèd Moon, with one bright star
Within the nether tip.

' One after one, by the star-dogg'd Moon,
Too quick for groan or sigh,
Each turn'd his face with a ghastly pang,
And cursed me with his eye.

dogg'd] followed closely by,

' Four times fifty living men,
(And I heard nor sigh nor groan)
With heavy thump, a lifeless lump,
They dropt down one by one.

' The souls did from their bodies fly,—
They fled to bliss or woe !
And every soul, it pass'd me by
Like the whizz of my cross-bow.'

Part IV

' I fear thee, ancient Mariner !
I fear thy skinny hand !
And thou art long, and lank, and brown,
As is the ribb'd sea-sand.

' I fear thee and thy glittering eye,
And thy skinny hand so brown.'
—' Fear not, fear not, thou Wedding-Guest !
This body dropt not down.

' Alone, alone, all, all alone,
Alone on a wide, wide sea !
And never a saint took pity on
My soul in agony.

' The many men, so beautiful !
And they all dead did lie :
And a thousand thousand slimy things
Lived on ; and so did I.

' I look'd upon the rotting sea,
And drew my eyes away ;
I look'd upon the rotting deck,
And there the dead men lay.

'I look'd to heaven, and tried to pray ;
But or ever a prayer had gusht,
A wicked whisper came, and made
My heart as dry as dust.

'I closed my lids, and kept them close,
And the balls like pulses beat ;
For the sky and the sea, and the sea and the sky
Lay like a load on my weary eye,
And the dead were at my feet.

'The cold sweat melted from their limbs,
Nor rot nor reek did they :
The look with which they look'd on me
Had never pass'd away.

'An orphan's curse would drag to Hell
A spirit from on high ;
But oh ! more horrible than that
Is the curse in a dead man's eye !
Seven days, seven nights, I saw that curse,
And yet I could not die.

'The moving Moon went up the sky,
And nowhere did abide :
Softly she was going up,
And a star or two beside—

'Her beams bemock'd the sultry main,
Like April hoar-frost spread ;
But where the ship's huge shadow lay,
The charmèd water burnt alway
A still and awful red.

'Beyond the shadow of the ship,
I watch'd the water-snakes :
They moved in tracks of shining white,
And when they rear'd, the elfish light
Fell off in hoary flakes.

D

' Within the shadow of the ship
I watch'd their rich attire :
Blue, glossy green, and velvet black,
They coil'd and swam ; and every track
Was a flash of golden fire.

' O happy living things ! no tongue
Their beauty might declare :
A spring of love gush'd from my heart,
And I bless'd them unaware :
Sure my kind saint took pity on me,
And I bless'd them unaware.

' The selfsame moment I could pray ;
And from my neck so free
The Albatross fell off, and sank
Like lead into the sea.

PART V

' O sleep ! it is a gentle thing,
Beloved from pole to pole !
To Mary Queen the praise be given !
She sent the gentle sleep from Heaven
That slid into my soul.

' The silly buckets on the deck
That had so long remain'd,
I dreamt that they were fill'd with dew ;
And when I awoke, it rain'd.

' My lips were wet, my throat was cold,
My garments all were dank ;
Sure I had drunken in my dreams,
And still my body drank.

' I moved, and could not feel my limbs :
I was so light—almost
I thought that I had died in sleep,
And was a blessèd ghost.

' And soon I heard a roaring wind :
It did not come anear ;
But with its sound it shook the sails,
That were so thin and sere.

' The upper air burst into life !
And a hundred fire-flags sheen,
To and fro, they were hurried about ;
And to and fro, and in and out,
The wan stars danced between.

' And the coming wind did roar more loud,
And the sails did sigh like sedge ;
And the rain pour'd down from one black cloud ;
The Moon was at its edge.

' The thick black cloud was cleft, and still
The Moon was at its side :
Like waters shot from some high crag,
The lightning fell with never a jag,
A river steep and wide.

' The loud wind never reach'd the ship,
Yet now the ship moved on !
Beneath the lightning and the Moon
The dead men gave a groan.

' They groan'd, they stirr'd, they all uprose,
Nor spake, nor moved their eyes ;
It had been strange, e'en in a dream,
To have seen those dead men rise.

sere] withered and dry.　　sheen] adj., bright.　　wan] pale.

'The helmsman steer'd ; the ship moved on ;
Yet never a breeze up-blew ;
The mariners all gan work the ropes,
Where they were wont to do ;
They raised their limbs like lifeless tools—
We were a ghastly crew.

' The body of my brother's son
Stood by me, knee to knee :
The body and I pull'd at one rope,
But he said nought to me.'

—' I fear thee, ancient Mariner ! '
—' Be calm, thou Wedding-Guest !
'Twas not those souls that fled in pain
Which to their corses came again,
But a troop of spirits blest :

' For when it dawn'd they dropp'd their arms,
And cluster'd round the mast ;
Sweet sounds rose slowly through their mouths,
And from their bodies pass'd.

' Around, around, flew each sweet sound,
Then darted to the Sun ;
Slowly the sounds came back again,
Now mix'd, now one by one.

' Sometimes a-dropping from the sky
I heard the skylark sing ;
Sometimes all little birds that are,
How they seem'd to fill the sea and air
With their sweet jargoning !

corses] corpses.   jargoning] warbling.

' And now 'twas like all instruments,
Now like a lonely flute ;
And now it is an angel's song,
That makes the heavens be mute.

' It ceased ; yet still the sails made on
A pleasant noise till noon,
A noise like of a hidden brook
In the leafy month of June,
That to the sleeping woods all night
Singeth a quiet tune.

' Till noon we quietly sail'd on,
Yet never a breeze did breathe :
Slowly and smoothly went the ship,
Moved onward from beneath.

' Under the keel nine fathom deep,
From the land of mist and snow,
The Spirit slid ; and it was he
That made the ship to go.
The sails at noon left off their tune,
And the ship stood still also.

' The Sun, right up above the mast,
Had fix'd her to the ocean :
But in a minute she gan stir,
With a short uneasy motion—
Backwards and forwards half her length,
With a short uneasy motion.

' Then like a pawing horse let go,
She made a sudden bound :
It flung the blood into my head,
And I fell down in a swound.

' How long in that same fit I lay,
I have not to declare ;
But ere my living life return'd,
I heard, and in my soul discern'd
Two voices in the air.

' " Is it he ? " quoth one, " is this the man ?
By Him who died on cross,
With his cruel bow he laid full low
The harmless Albatross.

' " The Spirit who bideth by himself
In the land of mist and snow,
He loved the bird that loved the man
Who shot him with his bow."

' The other was a softer voice,
As soft as honey-dew :
Quoth he, " The man hath penance done,
And penance more will do."

Part VI

First Voice

' " But tell me, tell me ! speak again,
Thy soft response renewing—
What makes that ship drive on so fast ?
What is the Ocean doing ? "

Second Voice

' " Still as a slave before his lord,
The Ocean hath no blast ;
His great bright eye most silently
Up to the Moon is cast—

penance] punishment to do away sin.

' " If he may know which way to go ;
For she guides him smooth or grim.
See, brother, see ! how graciously
She looketh down on him."

First Voice
' " But why drives on that ship so fast,
Without or wave or wind ? "

Second Voice
' " The air is cut away before,
And closes from behind.
Fly, brother, fly ! more high, more high !
Or we shall be belated :
For slow and slow that ship will go,
When the Mariner's trance is abated."

' I woke, and we were sailing on
As in a gentle weather :
'Twas night, calm night, the Moon was high ;
The dead men stood together.

' All stood together on the deck,
For a charnel-dungeon fitter :
All fix'd on me their stony eyes,
That in the Moon did glitter.

' The pang, the curse with which they died,
Had never pass'd away :
I could not draw my eyes from theirs,
Nor turn them up to pray.

' And now this spell was snapt once **more** :
I view'd the ocean green,
And look'd far forth, yet little saw
Of what had else been seen—

'Like one that on a lonesome road
Doth walk in fear and dread,
And having once turn'd round, walks on,
And turns no more his head;
Because he knows a frightful fiend
Doth close behind him tread.

'But soon there breathed a wind on me,
Nor sound nor motion made:
Its path was not upon the sea,
In ripple or in shade.

'It raised my hair, it fann'd my cheek
Like a meadow-gale of spring—
It mingled strangely with my fears,
Yet it felt like a welcoming.

'Swiftly, swiftly flew the ship,
Yet she sail'd softly too:
Sweetly, sweetly blew the breeze—
On me alone it blew.

'Oh! dream of joy! is this indeed
The light-house top I see?
Is this the hill? is this the kirk?
Is this mine own countree?

'We drifted o'er the harbour-bar,
And I with sobs did pray—
O let me be awake, my God!
Or let me sleep alway.

'The harbour-bay was clear as glass,
So smoothly it was strewn!
And on the bay the moonlight lay,
And the shadow of the Moon.

'The rock shone bright, the kirk no less,
That stands above the rock :
The moonlight steep'd in silentness
The steady weathercock.

'And the bay was white with silent light,
Till, rising from the same,
Full many shapes, that shadows were,
In crimson colours came.

'A little distance from the prow
Those crimson shadows were :
I turn'd my eyes upon the deck—
O Christ ! what saw I there !

'Each corse lay flat, lifeless and flat,
And, by the holy rood !
A man all light, a seraph-man,
On every corse there stood.

'This seraph-band, each waved his hand :
It was a heavenly sight !
They stood as signals to the land,
Each one a lovely light :

'This seraph-band, each waved his hand,
No voice did they impart—
No voice ; but oh ! the silence sank
Like music on my heart.

'But soon I heard the dash of oars,
I heard the Pilot's cheer ;
My head was turn'd perforce away,
And I saw a boat appear.

'The Pilot and the Pilot's boy,
I heard them coming fast :
Dear Lord in Heaven ! it was a joy
The dead men could not blast.

'I saw a third—I heard his voice :
It is the Hermit good !
He singeth loud his godly hymns
That he makes in the wood.
He 'll shrieve my soul, he 'll wash away
The Albatross's blood.

Part VII

'This Hermit good lives in that wood
Which slopes down to the sea.
How loudly his sweet voice he rears !
He loves to talk with marineres
That come from a far countree.

'He kneels at morn, and noon, and eve—
He hath a cushion plump :
It is the moss that wholly hides
The rotted old oak-stump.

'The skiff-boat near'd : I heard them talk,
" Why, this is strange, I trow !
Where are those lights so many and fair,
That signal made but now ? "

'" Strange, by my faith," the Hermit said—
" And they answer'd not our cheer !
The planks look warp'd ! and see those sails,
How thin they are and sere !
I never saw aught like to them,
Unless perchance it were

blast] destroy.   shrieve] cleanse from sin.
trow] think truly * .

' " Brown skeletons of leaves that lag
My forest-brook along ;
When the ivy-tod is heavy with snow,
And the owlet whoops to the wolf below,
That eats the she-wolf's young."

' —" Dear Lord ! it hath a fiendish look "
(The Pilot made reply)
" I am a-fear'd."—" Push on, push on ! "
Said the Hermit cheerily.

' The boat came closer to the ship,
But I nor spake nor stirr'd ;
The boat came close beneath the ship,
And straight a sound was heard :—

' Under the water it rumbled on,
Still louder and more dread :
It reach'd the ship, it split the bay ;
The ship went down like lead.

' Stunn'd by that loud and dreadful sound,
Which sky and ocean smote,
Like one that hath been seven days drown'd
My body lay afloat ;
But swift as dreams, myself I found
Within the Pilot's boat.

' Upon the whirl, where sank the ship,
The boat spun round and round ;
And all was still, save that the hill
Was telling of the sound.

' I moved my lips—the Pilot shriek'd
And fell down in a fit :
The holy Hermit raised his eyes,
And pray'd where he did sit.

tod] bush

' I took the oars : the Pilot's boy,
Who now doth crazy go,
Laugh'd loud and long, and all the while
His eyes went to and fro.
" Ha ! ha ! " quoth he, " full plain I see
The Devil knows how to row."

' And now, all in my own countree,
I stood on the firm land !
The Hermit stepp'd forth from the boat,
And scarcely he could stand.

' " O shrieve me, shrieve me, holy man ! "
The Hermit cross'd his brow,
" Say quick," quoth he, " I bid thee say—
What manner of man art thou ? "

' Forthwith this frame of mine was wrench'd
With a woful agony,
Which forced me to begin my tale ;
And then it left me free.

' Since then, at an uncertain hour,
That agony returns :
And till my ghastly tale is told,
This heart within me burns.

' I pass, like night, from land to land ;
I have strange power of speech ;
That moment that his face I see,
I know the man that must hear me :
To him my tale I teach.

' —What loud uproar bursts from that door !
The wedding guests are there :
But in the garden-bower the bride
And bridesmaids singing are :
And hark the little vesper bell,
Which biddeth me to prayer !

'O Wedding-Guest! this soul hath been
Alone on a wide, wide sea :
So lonely 'twas, that God Himself
Scarce seemèd there to be.

'O sweeter than the marriage-feast,
'Tis sweeter far to me,
To walk together to the kirk
With a goodly company !—

'To walk together to the kirk,
And all together pray,
While each to his great Father bends,
Old men, and babes, and loving friends,
And youths and maidens gay !

'—Farewell, farewell ! but this I tell
To thee, thou Wedding-Guest !
He prayeth well who loveth well
Both man and bird and beast.

'He prayeth best, who loveth best
All things both great and small ;
For the dear God who loveth us,
He made and loveth all.'

—The Mariner, whose eye is bright,
Whose beard with age is hoar,
Is gone : and now the Wedding-Guest
Turn'd from the bridegroom's door.

He went like one that hath been stunn'd,
And is of sense forlorn :
A sadder and a wiser man,
He rose the morrow morn.

Coleridge.

49   *The Snare*

I HEAR a sudden cry of pain !
    There is a rabbit in a snare :
Now I hear the cry again,
    But I cannot tell from where.

But I cannot tell from where
    He is calling out for aid ;
Crying on the frighten'd air,
    Making everything afraid.

Making everything afraid,
    Wrinkling up his little face,
As he cries again for aid ;
    And I cannot find the place !

And I cannot find the place
    Where his paw is in the snare :
Little one ! Oh, little one !
    I am searching everywhere !

James Stephens.

50   *The Reverie of Poor Susan*

AT the corner of Wood Street, when daylight appears,
Hangs a Thrush that sings loud, it has sung for three
    years :
Poor Susan has pass'd by the spot, and has heard
In the silence of morning the song of the Bird.

'Tis a note of enchantment ; what ails her ? She sees
A mountain ascending, a vision of trees ;
Bright volumes of vapour through Lothbury glide,
And a river flows on through the vale of Cheapside.

Lothbury] *oth* pronounced as in *both.*

Green pastures she views in the midst of the dale,
Down which she so often has tripp'd with her pail ;
And a single small cottage, a nest like a dove's,
The one only dwelling on earth that she loves.

She looks, and her heart is in heaven : but they fade,
The mist and the river, the hill and the shade :
The stream will not flow, and the hill will not rise,
And the colours have all pass'd away from her eyes !

Wordsworth, 1797.

51

    A WIDOW bird sate mourning for her love
        Upon a wintry bough ;
    The frozen wind crept on above,
        The freezing stream below.

    There was no leaf upon the forest bare,
        No flower upon the ground,
    And little motion in the air
        Except the mill-wheel's sound.

Shelley.

52*   *The Recollection*

I

    WE wander'd to the Pine Forest
        That skirts the Ocean's foam,
    The lightest wind was in its nest,
        The tempest in its home.
    The whispering waves were half asleep,
        The clouds were gone to play,
    And on the bosom of the deep
        The smile of Heaven lay ;

It seem'd as if the hour were one
　Sent from beyond the skies,
Which scatter'd from above the sun
　A light of Paradise.

II

We paused amid the pines that stood
　The giants of the waste,
Tortured by storms to shapes as rude
　As serpents interlaced,
And soothed by every azure breath
　That under Heaven is blown,
To harmonies and hues beneath,
　As tender as its own ;
Now all the tree-tops lay asleep,
　Like green waves on the sea,
As still as in the silent deep
　The ocean woods may be.

III

How calm it was !—the silence there
　By such a chain was bound
That even the busy woodpecker
　Made stiller by her sound
The inviolable quietness ;
　The breath of peace we drew
With its soft motion made not less
　The calm that round us grew.
There seem'd from the remotest seat
　Of the white mountain waste,
To the soft flower beneath our feet,
　A magic circle traced,—
A spirit interfused around,
　A thrilling, silent life,—
To momentary peace it bound
　Our mortal nature's strife ;

And still I felt the centre of
  The magic circle there
Was one fair form that fill'd with love
  The lifeless atmosphere.

IV

We paused beside the pools that lie
  Under the forest bough,—
Each seem'd as 'twere a little sky
  Gulf'd in a world below ;
A firmament of purple light
  Which in the dark earth lay,
More boundless than the depth of night,
  And purer than the day—
In which the lovely forests grew,
  As in the upper air,
More perfect both in shape and hue
  Than any spreading there.
There lay the glade and neighbouring lawn,
  And through the dark green wood
The white sun twinkling like the dawn
  Out of a speckled cloud.
Sweet views which in our world above
  Can never well be seen,
Were imaged by the water's love
  Of that fair forest green.
And all was interfused beneath
  With an Elysian glow,
An atmosphere without a breath,
  A softer day below.
Like one beloved the scene had lent
  To the dark water's breast
Its every leaf and lineament
  With more than truth express'd ;

Elysian] Elysium in Greek mythology was the abode of the blessed
after death.   lineament] outline.

E

Until an envious wind crept by,
   Like an unwelcome thought,
Which from the mind's too faithful eye
   Blots one dear image out.
Though thou art ever fair and kind,
   The forests ever green,
Less oft is peace in Shelley's mind,
   Than calm in waters, seen.

Shelley.

53   *Kubla Khan; or, A Vision in a Dream*

In Xanadu did Kubla Khan
A stately pleasure-dome decree :
Where Alph, the sacred river, ran
Through caverns measureless to man
   Down to a sunless sea.
So twice five miles of fertile ground
With walls and towers were girdled round :
And there were gardens bright with sinuous rills
Where blossom'd many an incense-bearing tree ;
And here were forests ancient as the hills,
Enfolding sunny spots of greenery.

But O ! that deep romantic chasm which slanted
Down the green hill athwart a cedarn cover !
A savage place ! as holy and enchanted
As e'er beneath a waning moon was haunted
By woman wailing for her demon-lover !
And from this chasm, with ceaseless turmoil seething,
As if this earth in fast thick pants were breathing,
A mighty fountain momently was forced :

     sinuous] winding.

Amid whose swift half-intermitted burst
Huge fragments vaulted like rebounding hail,
Or chaffy grain beneath the thresher's flail :
And 'mid these dancing rocks at once and ever
It flung up momently the sacred river.
Five miles meandering with a mazy motion
Through wood and dale the sacred river ran,
Then reach'd the caverns measureless to man,
And sank in tumult to a lifeless ocean :
And 'mid this tumult Kubla heard from far
Ancestral voices prophesying war !

The shadow of the dome of pleasure
Floated midway on the waves ;
Where was heard the mingled measure
From the fountain and the caves.
It was a miracle of rare device,
A sunny pleasure-dome with caves of ice !

A damsel with a dulcimer
In a vision once I saw :
It was an Abyssinian maid,
And on her dulcimer she play'd,
Singing of Mount Abora.
Could I revive within me
Her symphony and song,
To such a deep delight 'twould win me,
That with music loud and long,
I would build that dome in air,
That sunny dome ! those caves of ice !
And all who heard should see them there,
And all should cry, Beware ! Beware !
His flashing eyes, his floating hair !

intermitted] interrupted.   measure] rhythm as of music.
dulcimer] a percussion instrument, whether of stretched strings or
of bars,   symphony] accompaniment.

Weave a circle round him thrice,
And close your eyes with holy dread,
For he on honey-dew hath fed,
And drunk the milk of Paradise.

Coleridge, 1797.

54

SWEEP thy faint strings, Musician,
  With thy long lean hand ;
Downward the starry tapers burn,
  Sinks soft the waning sand ;
The old hound whimpers couch'd in sleep,
  The embers smoulder low ;
Across the wall the shadows
  Come, and go.

Sweep softly thy strings, Musician,
  The minutes mount to hours ;
Frost on the windless casement weaves
  A labyrinth of flowers ;
Ghosts linger in the darkening air,
  Hearken at the open door ;
Music hath call'd them, dreaming,
  Home once more.

Walter de la Mare.

55   *The Ballad of True Thomas*

TRUE Thomas lay on Huntlie bank ;
  A ferlie he spied wi' his ee ;
And there he saw a lady bright
  Come riding down by the Eildon Tree.

ferlie] marvel.   Eildon Tree] under which Thomas the Rhymer
delivered his prophecies.

Her skirt was o' the grass-green silk,
    Her mantle o' the velvet fine ;
At ilka tett of her horse's mane
    Hung fifty siller bells and nine.

True Thomas he pu'd aff his cap
    And louted low down to his knee :
' All hail, thou mighty Queen of heaven !
    For thy peer on earth I never did see.'

' O no, O no, Thomas (she said),
    That name does not belang to me ;
I 'm but the Queen o' fair Elfland,
    That am hither come to visit thee.

' Harp and carp, Thomas (she said) ;
    Harp and carp along wi' me ;
And if ye dare to kiss my lips,
    Sure of your bodie I will be.'—

' Betide me weal, betide me woe,
    That weird shall never daunten me.'
Syne he has kiss'd her rosy lips,
    All underneath the Eildon Tree.

' Now ye maun go wi' me (she said),
    True Thomas, ye maun go wi' me ;
And ye maun serve me seven years,
    Thro' weal or woe as may chance to be.'

She mounted on her milk-white steed,
    She 's ta'en true Thomas up behind :
And aye, whene'er her bridle rang,
    The steed flew swifter than the wind.

ilka tett] every tassel.   harp and carp] play and recite.
weird] fate.   syne] then.

O they rade on, and farther on,
   The steed gaed swifter than the wind :
Until they reach'd a desert wide,
   And living land was left behind.

' Light down, light down now, true Thomas,
   And lean your head upon my knee :
Abide and rest a little space,
   And I will show you ferlies three.

' O see ye not yon narrow road,
   So thick beset wi' thorns and briers ?
That is the Path of Righteousness,
   Tho' after it but few enquires.

' And see ye not that braid braid road,
   That lies across yon lily leven ?
That is the Path of Wickedness,
   Tho' some call it the Road to Heaven.

' And see ye not that bonny road
   That winds about the fernie brae ?
That is the Road to fair Elfland,
   Where thou and I this night maun gae.

' But, Thomas, ye sall haud your tongue,
   Whatever ye may hear or see :
For if ye speak word in Elflyn-land,
   Ye 'll ne'er get back to your ain countrie.'

O they rade on, and farther on,
   And they waded thro' rivers abune the knee :
And they saw neither sun nor mune,
   But they heard the roaring of the sea.

lily leven] flowery lawn.   brae] hillside.   abune] above.

It was mirk mirk night, there was nae sternlight,
   They waded thro' red blude to the knee :
For a' the blude that 's shed on earth
   Rins thro' the springs o' that countrie.

Syne they came to a garden green,
   And she pu'd an apple frae a tree :
' Take this for thy wages, true Thomas ;
   It will give the tongue that can never lee.'—

' My tongue is mine ain (true Thomas said) :
   A gudely gift ye wad gie to me !
I neither dought to buy nor sell
   At fair or tryst where I may be.

' I dought neither speak to prince or peer,
   Nor ask of grace from fair ladye ! '—
' Now hold thy peace, Thomas (she said),
   For as I say, so must it be.'

He has gotten a coat of the even cloth
   And a pair o' shoon o' the velvet green :
And till seven years were gane and past,
   True Thomas on earth was never seen.

56* *The Wife of Usher's Well*

   THERE lived a wife at Usher's well,
      And a wealthy wife was she ;
   She had three stout and stalwart sons,
      And sent them o'er the sea.

mirk] dark.   dought] could.   even] smooth.

They hadna been a week from her,
  A week but barely ane,
When word came to the carline wife
  That her three sons were gane.

They hadna been a week from her,
  A week but barely three,
When word came to the carline wife
  That her sons she 'd never see.

' I wish the wind may never cease,
  Nor fashes in the flood,
Till my three sons come hame to me
  In earthly flesh and blood ! '

It fell about the Martinmas,
  When nights are lang and mirk,
The carline wife's three sons came hame,
  And their hats were o' the birk.

It neither grew in syke nor ditch,
  Nor yet in ony sheugh ;
But at the gates o' Paradise
  That birk grew fair eneugh.

' Blow up the fire, my maidens !
  Bring water from the well !
For a' my house shall feast this night,
  Since my three sons are well.'

And she has made to them a bed,
  She 's made it large and wide ;
And she 's ta'en her mantle her about,
  Sat down at the bedside.

carline] stout old woman.   fashes] troubles.   Martinmas]*.
birk] birch.   syke] ditch.   sheugh] trench

Up then crew the red, red cock,
　And up and crew the gray ;
The eldest to the youngest said,
　‘ 'Tis time we were away.’

The cock he hadna craw’d but once,
　And clapp’d his wings at a’,
When the youngest to the eldest said,
　‘ Brother, we must awa'.

‘ The cock doth craw, the day doth daw,
　The channerin' worm doth chide ;
Gin we be miss’d out of our place,
　A sair pain we maun bide.’

‘ Lie still, lie still but a little wee while,
　Lie still but if we may ;
Gin my mother should miss us when she wakes,
　She ’ll go mad ere it be day.’

‘ Fare ye weel, my mother dear !
　Fareweel to barn and byre !
And fare ye weel, the bonny lass
　That kindles my mother’s fire ! ’

57　　*Helen of Kirconnell*

I wish I were where Helen lies,
Night and day on me she cries :
O that I were where Helen lies,
　On fair Kirconnell lea !

Curst be the heart that thought the thought,
And curst the hand that fired the shot,
When in my arms burd Helen dropt,
　And died to succour me !

channering] fretting.　　gin] if.　　byre] cowhouse.
burd] maiden, lady.

O think na ye my heart was sair,
When my Love dropt and spak nae mair ?
There did she swoon wi' meikle care,
   On fair Kirconnell lea.

As I went down the waterside
None but my foe to be my guide,
None but my foe to be my guide,
   On fair Kirconnell lea ;

I lighted down, my sword did draw,
I hackèd him in pieces sma',
I hackèd him in pieces sma',
   For her sake that died for me.

O Helen fair beyond compare !
I 'll make a garland of thy hair,
Shall bind my heart for evermair
   Until the day I dee.

O that I were where Helen lies !
Night and day on me she cries ;
Out of my bed she bids me rise,
   Says, ' Haste and come to me.'

O Helen fair !   O Helen chaste !
If I were with thee I were blest,
Where thou lies low, and takes thy rest
   On fair Kirconnell lea.

I wish my grave were growing green,
A winding sheet drawn owre my een,
And I in Helen's arms lying
   On fair Kirconnell lea.

I wish I were where Helen lies !
Night and day on me she cries :
And I am weary of the skies
   For her sake that died for me.

      meikle] much, also mickle, muckle.

58   *The Sands of Dee*

I

' O Mary, go and call the cattle home,
     And call the cattle home,
     And call the cattle home
    Across the Sands of Dee.'
The western wind was wild and dank with foam,
     And all alone went she.

II

The western tide crept up along the sand,
     And o'er and o'er the sand,
     And round and round the sand,
    As far as eye could see.
The rolling mist came down and hid the land ;
     And never home came she.

III

' Oh ! is it weed, or fish, or floating hair—
     A tress of golden hair,
     A drownèd maiden's hair
    Above the nets at sea ? '
Was never salmon yet that shone so fair
     Among the stakes on Dee.

IV

They row'd her in across the rolling foam,
     The cruel crawling foam,
     The cruel hungry foam,
    To her grave beside the sea :
But still the boatmen hear her call the cattle home
    Across the Sands of Dee.

Kingsley.

59   *Auld Robin Gray*

WHEN the sheep are in the fauld, and the kye at hame,
And a' the warld to rest are gane,
The waes o' my heart fa' in showers frae my ee,
While my gudeman lies sound by me.

Young Jamie lo'ed me weel, and sought me for his bride;
But saving a croun he had naething else beside :
To make the croun a pund, young Jamie gaed to sea ;
And the croun and the pund were baith for me.

He hadna been awa' a week but only twa,
When my father brak his arm, and the cow was stown
     awa' ;
My mother she fell sick, and my Jamie at the sea—
And auld Robin Gray came a-courtin' me.

My father couldna work, and my mother couldna spin ;
I toil'd day and night, but their bread I couldna win ;
Auld Rob maintain'd them baith, and wi' tears in his ee
Said, ' Jennie, for their sakes, O, marry me ! '

My heart it said nay ; I look'd for Jamie back ;
But the wind it blew high, and the ship it was a wrack ;
His ship it was a wrack—why didna Jamie dee ?
Or why do I live to cry, Wae 's me ?

My father urgit sair : my mother didna speak ;
But she look'd in my face till my heart was like to break :
They gie'd him my hand, but my heart was at the sea :
Sae auld Robin Gray he was gudeman to me.

fauld] fold.	kye] cattle.	fa'] fall.
gaed] went.	a week but . . .] a fortnight.	stown] stolen.
dee] die.	urgit]'pressed.	gudeman] husband.

I hadna been a wife a week but only four,
When mournfu' as I sat on the stane at the door,
I saw my Jamie's wraith, for I couldna think it he—
Till he said, ' I 'm come hame to marry thee.'

—O sair, sair did we greet, and muckle did we say ;
We took but ae kiss, and I bad him gang away :
I wish that I were dead, but I 'm no like to dee ;
And why was I born to say, Wae 's me !

I gang like a ghaist, and I carena to spin ;
I daurna think on Jamie, for that wad be a sin ;
But I 'll do my best a gude wife aye to be,
For auld Robin Gray he is kind unto me.

Lady Lindsay.

60

O, my love 's like a red, red rose,
    That 's newly sprung in June :
O, my love 's like the melody
    That 's sweetly play'd in tune.

As fair art thou, my bonnie lass,
    So deep in love am I :
And I will love thee still, my dear,
    Till a' the seas gang dry.

Till a' the seas gang dry, my dear,
    And the rocks melt wi' the sun !
And I will love thee still, my dear,
    While the sands o' life shall run.

And fare thee well, my only love,
    And fare thee well a-while !
And I will come again, my love,
    Tho' it were ten thousand mile !

Burns.*

wraith] ghost.   sair] sorely.   greet] cry.
muckle] much.   daurna] dare not.

61   *John Anderson*

JOHN ANDERSON, my jo, John,
    When we were first acquent,
Your locks were like the raven,
    Your bonnie brow was brent ;
But now your brow is beld, John,
    Your locks are like the snow :
But blessings on your frosty pow,
    John Anderson, my jo !

John Anderson, my jo, John,
    We clamb the hill tegither ;
And mony a canty day, John,
    We 've had wi' ane anither :
Now we maun totter down, John,
    But hand in hand we 'll go ;
And sleep tegither at the foot,
    John Anderson, my jo.

Burns.

62   *The Land o' the Leal*

I 'M wearin' awa', John,
Like snaw-wreaths in thaw, John,
I 'm wearin' awa'
    To the land o' the leal.
There 's nae sorrow there, John,
There 's neither cauld nor care, John,
The day is aye fair
    In the land o' the leal.

Our bonnie bairn 's there, John,
She was baith gude and fair, John ;
And O ! we grudged her sair
    To the land o' the leal.

brent] smooth, unwrinkled.   beld] bald.
pow] pate.   canty] cheerful.

But sorrow's sel' wears past, John,
And joy 's a-coming fast, John,
The joy that 's aye to last
  In the land o' the leal.

Sae dear 's the joy was bought, John,
Sae free the battle fought, John,
That sinfu' man e'er brought
  To the land o' the leal.
O, dry your glistening ee, John !
My saul langs to be free, John,
And angels beckon me
  To the land o' the leal.

O, haud ye leal and true, John !
Your day it 's wearin' through, John,
And I 'll welcome you
  To the land o' the leal.
Now fare-ye-weel, my ain John,
This warld's cares are vain, John,
We 'll meet, and we 'll be fain,
  In the land o' the leal.

Lady Nairne.

63   *The Farewell*

It was a' for our rightfu' King
  We left fair Scotland's strand ;
It was a' for our rightfu' King
  We e'er saw Irish land,
      My dear—
  We e'er saw Irish land.

Now a' is done that men can do,
  And a' is done in vain ;
My love and native land, farewell !
  For I maun cross the main,
      My dear—
  For I maun cross the main.

He turn'd him right and round about
  Upon the Irish shore ;
And gae his bridle-reins a shake,
  With Adieu for evermore,
      My dear—
  With Adieu for evermore !

The sodger frae the wars returns,
  The sailor frae the main ;
But I hae parted frae my love,
  Never to meet again,
      My dear—
  Never to meet again.

When day is gane, and night is come,
  And a' folk bound to sleep,
I think on him that 's far awa',
  The lee-lang night, and weep,
      My dear—
  The lee-lang night, and weep.

*Old Song.**

64   *There 'll never be Peace*

By yon castle wa', at the close of the day,
I heard a man sing, tho' his head it was grey ;
And as he was singing, the tears fast down came,
There 'll never be peace till Jamie comes hame.

main] the high sea.   lee-lang] live-long.

The Church is in ruins, the State is in jars,
Delusions, oppressions, and murderous wars :
We darena weel say 't, tho' we ken wha 's to blame—
There 'll never be peace till Jamie comes hame.

My seven braw sons for Jamie drew sword,
And now I greet round their green beds in the yerd.
It brak the sweet heart of my faithful auld dame—
There 'll never be peace till Jamie comes hame.

Now life is a burden that bows me down,
Sin' I tint my bairns, and he tint his crown ;
But till my last moments my words are the same—
There 'll never be peace till Jamie comes hame.

Burns.

65   *Cock up your Beaver*

WHEN first my brave Johnnie lad
    Came to this town,
He had a blue bonnet
    That wanted the crown ;
But now he has gotten
    A hat and a feather,—
Hey, brave Johnnie lad,
    Cock up your beaver !

Cock up your beaver,
    And cock it fu' sprush,
We 'll over the border
    And gie them a brush :
There 's somebody there
    We 'll teach better behaviour—
Hey, brave Johnnie lad,
    Cock up your beaver !

Burns.

braw] handsome.   greet] weep.   tint] lost.
beaver] hat.   sprush] spruce.

F

66   *Wee Willie Gray*

WEE Willie Gray, and his leather wallet ;
Peel a willow-wand to be him boots and jacket :
The rose upon the brier will be him trouse and doublet,
The rose upon the brier will be him trouse and doublet.

Wee Willie Gray, and his leather wallet ;
Twice a lily flower will be him sark and cravat :
Feathers of a flea wad feather up his bonnet,
Feathers of a flea wad feather up his bonnet.

Burns.

67   *To a Mouse*

WEE, sleekit, cow'rin', tim'rous beastie,
O what a panic 's in thy breastie !
Thou need na start awa' sae hasty,
      Wi' bickering brattle !
I wad be laith to rin an' chase thee
      Wi' murd'ring pattle !

I 'm truly sorry man's dominion
Has broken Nature's social union,
An' justifies that ill opinion
      Which mak's thee startle
At me, thy poor earth-born companion,
      An' fellow-mortal !

I doubt na, whiles, but thou may thieve ;
What then ? poor beastie, thou maun live !
A daimen-icker in a thrave
      'S a sma' request :
I 'll get a blessin' wi' the lave,
      And never miss 't !

sark] shirt.
pattle] plough-spade.
thrave] two dozen sheaves.

bickering brattle] scurrying rush.
daimen-icker] odd ear of corn.
lave] remainder.

Thy wee bit housie, too, in ruin !
Its silly wa's the win's are strewin' !
An' naething, now, to big a new ane,
      O' foggage green !
An' bleak December's winds ensuin',
      Baith snell an' keen !

Thou saw the fields laid bare and waste,
An' weary winter comin' fast,
An' cozie here, beneath the blast,
      Thou thought to dwell,
Till crash ! the cruel coulter pass'd
      Out thro' thy cell.

That wee bit heap o' leaves an' stibble
Has cost thee mony a weary nibble !
Now thou 's turn'd out, for a' thy trouble,
      But house or hald,
To thole the winter's sleety dribble,
      An' cranreuch cauld !

But, Mousie, thou art no thy lane
In proving foresight may be vain :
The best laid schemes o' mice an' men
      Gang aft a-gley,
An' lea'e us nought but grief an' pain
      For promis'd joy.

Still thou art blest, compar'd wi' me !
The present only toucheth thee :
But, och ! I backward cast my ee
      On prospects drear !
An' forward tho' I canna see,
      I guess an' fear !

                        Burns, 1785.

foggage] aftermath.	snell] biting.	but] without.
hald] hold, shelter.	thole] bear.	cranreuch] hoar-frost.
thy lane] alone.	a-gley] awry.	

68

HERE 's a health to them that 's away,
Here 's a health to them that 's away,
Here 's a health to them that were here short syne,
But canna be here the day.
It 's guid to be merry and wise,
It 's guid to be honest and true ;
It 's guid to be aff wi' the auld luve
Before ye be on wi' the new.

*Old Song.**

69* *True Worth*

. . . Honour and shame from no condition rise ;
Act well your part, there all the honour lies.
Fortune in men has some small difference made,
One flaunts in rags, one flutters in brocade ;
The cobbler apron'd, and the parson gown'd,
The friar hooded, and the monarch crown'd.
' What differ more (you cry) than crown and cowl ? '
I 'll tell you, friend ! a wise man and a fool.
You 'll find, if once the monarch acts the monk,
Or, cobbler-like, the parson will be drunk,
Worth makes the man, and want of it the fellow ;
The rest is all but leather or prunella. . . .

Pope.

70* *A Man's a Man for a' that*

Is there for honest poverty
    That hangs his head, and a' that ?
The coward slave, we pass him by,
    We dare be poor for a' that !

short syne] a short time ago.   but] nothing but.
prunella] the stuff the parson's gown was made of.
Is there] Is there any one who hangs . . .

For a' that, and a' that,
   Our toils obscure, and a' that ;
The rank is but the guinea stamp,
   The man 's the gowd for a' that !

What tho' on hamely fare we dine,
   Wear hoddin grey, and a' that ;
Gie fools their silks, and knaves their wine,
   A man 's a man for a' that :
For a' that, and a' that,
   Their tinsel show, and a' that,
The honest man, though e'er sae poor,
   Is king o' men for a' that !

You see yon birkie, ca'd a lord,
   Wha struts, and stares, and a' that ;
Though hundreds worship at his word,
   He 's but a coof for a' that :
For a' that, and a' that,
   His riband, star, and a' that,
The man of independent mind,
   He looks and laughs at a' that !

A king can mak' a belted knight,
   A marquis, duke, and a' that ;
But an honest man 's aboon his might,
   Guid faith, he mauna fa' that ;
For a' that, and a' that,
   Their dignities, and a' that,
The pith o' sense and pride o' worth
   Are higher ranks than a' that !

Then let us pray that come it may—
   As come it will for a' that—
That sense and worth, o'er a' the earth,
   May bear the gree, and a' that ;

gowd] gold.   hoddin grey] coarse undyed woollen cloth.
birkie] fellow.   coof] ninny, fool.   aboon] above.
fa' that], take that in hand.   bear the gree] take the prize.

For a' that, and a' that,
　　It 's comin' yet, for a' that,
That man to man, the warld o'er,
　　Shall brothers be for a' that !

Burns.

71　　　　*Auld Lang Syne*

SHOULD auld acquaintance be forgot,
　　And never brought to min' ?
Should auld acquaintance be forgot,
　　And days o' lang syne ?
　　　　For auld lang syne, my dear,
　　　　For auld lang syne,
　　　　We 'll tak' a cup o' kindness yet
　　　　For auld lang syne.

We twa hae run about the braes,
　　And pu'd the gowans fine ;
But we 've wander'd mony a weary foot
　　Sin' auld lang syne.
　　　　For auld, etc.

We twa hae paidl't i' the burn,
　　Frae mornin' sun till dine ;
But seas between us braid hae roar'd
　　Sin' auld lang syne.
　　　　For auld, etc.

And here 's a hand, my trusty fiere,
　　And gie 's a hand o' thine ;
And we 'll tak' a right guid-willie waught
　　For auld lang syne.
　　　　For auld, etc.

gowans] daisies.　　　　　　　　fiere] fere, mate, comrade.
guid-willie waught], friendly draught.

And surely ye 'll be your pint-stoup,
   And surely I 'll be mine ;
And we 'll tak' a cup o' kindness yet
   For auld lang syne.
      For auld, etc.

Burns.

72 *The Song of the Western Men*
(1688)

A GOOD sword and a trusty hand !
   A merry heart and true !
King James's men shall understand
   What Cornish lads can do.

And have they fix'd the where and when ?
   And shall Trelawny die ?
Here 's twenty thousand Cornish men
   Will know the reason why !

Out spake the captain, brave and bold,—
   A merry wight was he ;
' If London Tower were Michael's hold,
   We 'll set Trelawny free !

' We 'll cross the Tamar, land to land,
   The Severn is no stay,
With one and all, and hand in hand,
   And who shall bid us nay ?

' And when we come to London Wall,
   A pleasant sight to view ;—
Come forth ! come forth, ye cowards all,
   Here 's men as good as you !

' Trelawny he 's in keep in hold,
    Trelawny he may die ;
But here 's twenty thousand Cornish bold
    Will know the reason why ! '

*Hawker.**

73*   *The Old Navy*

THE captain stood on the carronade : ' First lieutenant,'
    says he,
' Send all my merry men aft here, for they must list
    to me ;
I haven't the gift of the gab, my sons—because I 'm
    bred to the sea ;
That ship there is a Frenchman, who means to fight
    with we.
      And odds bobs, hammer and tongs, long as I 've
        been to sea,
      I 've fought 'gainst every odds—but I 've gain'd
        the victory !

' That ship there is a Frenchman, and if we don't
    take she,
'Tis a thousand bullets to one, that she will capture we ;
I haven't the gift of the gab, my boys ; so each man
    to his gun ;
If she 's not mine in half an hour, I 'll flog each mother's
    son.
      For odds bobs, hammer and tongs, long as I 've
        been to sea,
      I 've fought 'gainst every odds—and I 've gain'd
        the victory ! '

We fought for twenty minutes, when the Frenchman
    had enough ;
' I little thought,' said he, ' that your men were of such
    stuff ' ;

Our captain took the Frenchman's sword, a low bow
made to he ;
' I haven't the gift of the gab, monsieur, but polite I
wish to be.
    And odds bobs, hammer and tongs, long as I 've
      been to sea,
      I 've fought 'gainst every odds—and I 've gain'd
        the victory ! '

Our captain sent for all of us : ' My merry men,'
said he,
' I haven't the gift of the gab, my lads, but yet I
thankful be :
You 've done your duty handsomely, each man stood
to his gun ;
If you hadn't, you villains, as sure as day, I 'd have
flogg'd each mother's son,
    For odds bobs, hammer and tongs, as long as
      I 'm at sea,
      I 'll fight 'gainst every odds—and I 'll gain the
        victory ! '

Marryat.

74 *English Irregular :* '99–'02

Chant Pagan

Me that 'ave been what I 've been,
Me that 'ave gone where I 've gone,
Me that 'ave seen what I 've seen—
'Ow can I ever take on
With awful old England again,
An' 'ouses both sides of the street,
And 'edges two sides of the lane,
And the parson an' ' gentry ' between,
An' touchin' my 'at when we meet—
    Me that 'ave been what I 've been ?

Me that 'ave watch'd 'arf a world
'Eave up all shiny with dew,
Kopje on kop to the sun,
An' as soon as the mist let 'em through
Our 'elios winkin' like fun—
Three sides of a ninety-mile square,
Over valleys as big as a shire—
Are ye there?   Are ye there?   Are ye there?
An' then the blind drum of our fire . . .
An' I 'm rollin' 'is lawns for the Squire,
                    Me!

Me that 'ave rode through the dark
Forty mile often on end,
Along the Ma'ollisberg Range,
With only the stars for my mark
An' only the night for my friend,
An' things runnin' off as you pass,
An' things jumpin' up in the grass,
An' the silence, the shine an' the size
Of the 'igh, inexpressible skies. . . .
I am takin' some letters almost
As much as a mile to the post,
An' ' mind you come back with the change!'
                    Me!

Me that saw Barberton took
When we dropp'd through the clouds on their 'ead,
An' they 'ove the guns over and fled—
Me that was through Di'mond 'Ill,
An' Pieters an' Springs an' Belfast—
From Dundee to Vereeniging all!
Me that stuck out to the last
(An' five bloomin' bars on my chest)—
I am doin' my Sunday-school best,
By the 'elp of the Squire an' 'is wife
(Not to mention the 'ousemaid an' cook),

To come in an' 'ands up an' be still,
An' honestly work for my bread,
My livin' in that state of life
To which it shall please God to call
Me !

Me that 'ave follow'd my trade
In the place where the Lightnin's are made,
'Twixt the Rains and the Sun and the Moon;
Me that lay down an' got up
Three years an' the sky for my roof—
That 'ave ridden my 'unger an' thirst
Six thousand raw mile on the hoof,
With the Vaal and the Orange for cup,
An' the Brandwater Basin for dish,—
Oh ! it 's 'ard to be'ave as they wish
(Too 'ard, an' a little too soon),
I 'll 'ave to think over it first—
Me !

I will arise an' get 'ence ;—
I will trek South and make sure
If it 's only my fancy or not
That the sunshine of England is pale,
And the breezes of England are stale,
An' there 's somethin' gone small with the lot ;
For *I* know of a sun an' a wind,
An' some plains and a mountain be'ind,
An' some graves by a barb-wire fence ;
An' a Dutchman I 've fought 'oo might give
Me a job were I ever inclined,
To look in an' offsaddle and live
Where there 's neither a road nor a tree—
But only my Maker an' me,
And I think it will kill me or cure,
So I think I will go there and see.

Rudyard Kipling.

75* *A Publisher to his Client*

DEAR Doctor, I have read your play
Which is a good one in its way,—
Purges the eyes and moves the bowels,
And drenches handkerchiefs like towels
With tears, that, in a flux of grief,
Afford hysterical relief
To shatter'd nerves and quicken'd pulses,
Which your catastrophe convulses.

I like your moral and machinery ;
Your plot too has such scope for scenery ;
Your dialogue is apt and smart ;
The play's concoction full of art ;
Your hero raves, your heroine cries,
All stab, and everybody dies.
In short, your tragedy would be
The very thing to hear and see ;
And, for a piece of publication,
If I decline on this occasion,
It is not that I am not sensible
To merits in themselves ostensible,
But—and I grieve to speak it—plays
Are drugs—mere drugs, sir—now-a-days.
I had a heavy loss by ' Manuel,'—
Too lucky if it prove not annual,—
And Sotheby, with his ' Orestes,'
(Which by the by, the author's best is),
Has lain so very long on hand,
That I despair of all demand.
I 've advertised—but see my books !
Or only watch my shopman's looks !—
Still Ivan, Ina, and such lumber,
My back-shop glut, my shelves encumber.

There 's Byron too, who once did better,
Has sent me, folded in a letter,
A sort of—it 's no more a drama
Than Darnley, Ivan, or Kehama :
So alter'd since last year his pen is,
I think he 's lost his wits at Venice.
In short, sir, what with one and t'other,
I dare not venture on another.
I write in haste ; excuse each blunder ;
The coaches thro' the street so thunder !
My room 's so full—we 've Gifford here
Reading MS., with Hookham Frere,
Pronouncing on the nouns and particles
Of some of our forthcoming Articles.

The Quarterly—Ah, sir, if you
Had but the genius to review !—
A smart critique upon St. Helena,
Or if you only would but tell in a
Short compass what—but, to resume . . .
As I was saying, sir, the room—
The room 's so full of wits and bards,
Crabbes, Campbells, Crokers, Freres, and Wards,
And others, neither bards nor wits :—
My humble tenement admits
All persons in the dress of gent.,
From Mr. Hammond to Dog Dent.

A party dines with me to-day,
All clever men, who make their way :
Crabbe, Malcolm, Hamilton, and Chantrey
Are all partakers of my pantry.
They 're at this moment in discussion
On poor De Staël's late dissolution.
Her book, they say, was in advance—
Pray Heaven she tell the truth of France !

Thus run our time and tongues away ;—
But, to return, sir, to your play :
Sorry, sir, but I cannot deal,
Unless 'twere acted by O'Neill.
My hands so full, my head so busy,
I 'm almost dead, and always dizzy ;
And so with endless truth and hurry,
Dear Doctor I am yours
John Murray.
Byron, 1817.

76* *A Literary Poet to his Patron*

. . Come then, my friend, my genius !   Come along ;
O master of the poet, and the song !
And while the muse now stoops, or now ascends,
To man's low passions, or their glorious ends,
Teach me, like thee, in various nature wise,
To fall with dignity, with temper rise ;
Form'd by thy converse, happily to steer
From grave to gay, from lively to severe ;
Correct with spirit, eloquent with ease,
Intent to reason, or polite to please.
Oh ! while along the stream of time thy name
Expanded flies, and gathers all its fame ;
Say, shall my little bark attendant sail,
Pursue the triumph and partake the gale ?
When statesmen, heroes, kings, in dust repose,
Whose sons shall blush their fathers were thy foes,
Shall then this verse to future age pretend
Thou wert my guide, philosopher, and friend ?
That urged by thee, I turn'd the tuneful art
From sounds to things, from fancy to the heart ;
For wit's false mirror held up Nature's light ;
Show'd erring pride, WHATEVER IS, IS RIGHT ;

That REASON, PASSION, answer one great aim ;
That true SELF-LOVE and SOCIAL are the same ;
That VIRTUE only makes our bliss below ;
And all our knowledge is, OURSELVES TO KNOW.

Pope.

77 *If*

IF you can keep your head when all about you
  Are losing theirs and blaming it on you ;
If you can trust yourself when all men doubt you,
  But make allowance for their doubting too ;
If you can wait and not be tired by waiting,
  Or being lied about don't deal in lies,
Or being hated don't give way to hating,
  And yet don't look too good, nor talk too wise :

If you can dream—and not make dreams your master ;
  If you can think—and not make thoughts your aim ;
If you can meet with Triumph and Disaster
  And treat those two impostors just the same ;
If you can bear to hear the truth you 've spoken
  Twisted by knaves to make a trap for fools,
Or watch the things you gave your life to, broken,
  And stoop and build 'em up with worn-out tools :

If you can make one heap of all your winnings
  And risk it on one turn of pitch-and-toss,
And lose, and start again at your beginnings
  And never breathe a word about your loss ;
If you can force your heart and nerve and sinew
  To serve your turn long after they are gone,
And so hold on when there is nothing in you
  Except the Will which says to them : ' Hold on ! '

If you can talk with crowds and keep your virtue,
  Or walk with Kings—nor lose the common touch ;
If neither foes nor loving friends can hurt you ;
  If all men count with you, but none too much ;
If you can fill the unforgiving minute
  With sixty seconds' worth of distance run,
Yours is the Earth and everything that 's in it,
  And (which is more) you 'll be a Man, my son !
                                    Rudyard Kipling.

78   *Drake's Drum*

DRAKE he 's in his hammock an' a thousand mile away,
  (Capten, art tha sleepin' there below ?),
Slung atween the round shot in Nombre Dios Bay,
  An' dreamin' arl the time o' Plymouth Hoe.
Yarnder lumes the Island, yarnder lie the ships,
  Wi' sailor lads a-dancin' heel-an'-toe,
An' the shore-lights flashin', an' the night-tide dashin',
  He sees et arl so plainly as he saw et long ago.

Drake he was a Devon man, an' rüled the Devon seas,
  (Capten, art tha sleepin' there below ?),
Rovin' tho' his death fell, he went wi' heart at ease,
  An' dreamin' arl the time o' Plymouth Hoe.
' Take my drum to England, hang et by the shore,
  Strike et when your powder 's runnin' low ;
If the Dons sight Devon, I 'll quit the port o' Heaven
  An' drum them up the Channel as we drumm'd them
    long ago.'

Drake he 's in his hammock till the great Armada 's
    come,
  (Capten, art tha sleepin' there below ?),
Slung atween the round shot, listenin' for the drum,
  An' dreamin' arl the time o' Plymouth Hoe.

Call him on the deep sea, call him up the Sound,
  Call him when ye sail to meet the foe ;
Where the old trade 's plyin' an' the old flag flyin'
  They shall find him ware an' wakin', as they found
    him long ago !

Henry Newbolt.

79   *To-day*

(1914)

For all we have and are,
For all our children's fate,
Stand up and meet the war.
The Hun is at the gate !
Our world has pass'd away
In wantonness o'erthrown.
There is nothing left to-day
But steel and fire and stone.
  Though all we knew depart,
  The old Commandments stand :
  ' In courage keep your heart,
  In strength lift up your hand.'

Once more we hear the word
That sicken'd earth of old :
' No law except the Sword
Unsheathed and uncontrol'd ' ;
Once more it knits mankind,
Once more the nations go
To meet and break and bind
A crazed and driven foe.

Comfort, content, delight—
The ages' slow-bought gain,
They shrivel'd in a night,
Only ourselves remain

G

To face the naked days
In silent fortitude,
Through perils and dismays
Renew'd and re-renew'd.
   Though all we made depart,
   The old Commandments stand :
   ' In patience keep your heart,
   In strength lift up your hand.'

No easy hopes or lies
Shall bring us to our goal,
But iron sacrifice
Of body, will, and soul.
There is but one task for all—
For each one life to give.
Who stands if Freedom fall ?
Who dies if England live ?

Rudyard Kipling.

80   *Death the Leveller*

THE glories of our blood and state
   Are shadows, not substantial things ;
There is no armour against Fate ;
   Death lays his icy hand on kings :
      Sceptre and Crown
      Must tumble down,
   And in the dust be equal made
   With the poor crookèd scythe and spade.

Some men with swords may reap the field,
   And plant fresh laurels where they kill ;
But their strong nerves at last must yield ;
   They tame but one another still :
      Early or late
      They stoop to fate,
   And must give up their murmuring breath
   When they, pale captives, creep to death.

The garlands wither on your brow :
  Then boast no more your mighty deeds !
Upon Death's purple altar now
  See where the victor-victim bleeds.
    Your heads must come
    To the cold tomb :
  Only the actions of the just
  Smell sweet and blossom in their dust.

Shirley.

81   *Ozymandias*

I MET a traveller from an antique land
Who said : Two vast and trunkless legs of stone
Stand in the desert. . . . Near them, on the sand,
Half sunk, a shatter'd visage lies, whose frown,
And wrinkled lip, and sneer of cold command,
Tell that its sculptor well those passions read
Which yet survive, stamp'd on these lifeless things,
The hand that mock'd them, and the heart that fed :
And on the pedestal these words appear :
' My name is Ozymandias, king of kings :
Look on my works, ye Mighty, and despair ! '
Nothing beside remains. Round the decay
Of that colossal wreck, boundless and bare
The lone and level sands stretch far away.

Shelley.

82   *Alastor*

EARTH, ocean, air, belovèd brotherhood !
If our great Mother has imbued my soul
With aught of natural piety to feel
Your love, and recompense the boon with mine ;
If dewy morn, and odorous noon, and even,

With sunset and its gorgeous ministers,
And solemn midnight's tingling silentness ;
If autumn's hollow sighs in the sere wood,
And winter robing with pure snow and crowns
Of starry ice the grey grass and bare boughs ;
If spring's voluptuous pantings when she breathes
Her first sweet kisses, have been dear to me ;
If no bright bird, insect, or gentle beast
I consciously have injured, but still loved
And cherish'd these my kindred : then forgive
This boast, belovèd brethren, and withdraw
No portion of your wonted favour now !

Mother of this unfathomable world !
Favour my solemn song, for I have loved
Thee ever, and thee only ; I have watch'd
Thy shadow, and the darkness of thy steps,
And my heart ever gazes on the depth
Of thy deep mysteries.   I have made my bed
In charnels and on coffins, where black death
Keeps record of the trophies won from thee,
Hoping to still these obstinate questionings
Of thee and thine, by forcing some lone ghost
Thy messenger, to render up the tale
Of what we are.   In lone and silent hours,
When night makes a weird sound of its own stillness,
Like an inspired and desperate alchymist
Staking his very life on some dark hope,
Have I mix'd awful talk and asking looks
With my most innocent love, until strange tears
Uniting with those breathless kisses, made
Such magic as compels the charmèd night
To render up thy charge ; . . . and, though ne'er yet
Thou hast unveil'd thy inmost sanctuary,
Enough from incommunicable dream,
And twilight phantasms, and deep noon-day thought,

Has shone within me, that serenely now
And moveless, as a long-forgotten lyre
Suspended in the solitary dome
Of some mysterious and deserted fane,
I wait thy breath, Great Parent, that my strain
May modulate with murmurs of the air,
And motions of the forests and the sea,
And voice of living beings, and woven hymns
Of night and day, and the deep heart of man. . . .

Shelley.

83

To one who has been long in city pent,
  'Tis very sweet to look into the fair
  And open face of heaven,—to breathe a prayer
Full in the smile of the blue firmament.
Who is more happy, when, with heart's content,
  Fatigued he sinks into some pleasant lair
  Of wavy grass, and reads a debonair
And gentle tale of love and languishment?
Returning home at evening, with an ear
  Catching the notes of Philomel,—an eye
Watching the sailing cloudlet's bright career,
  He mourns that day so soon has glided by:
E'en like the passage of an angel's tear
  That falls through the clear ether silently.

Keats.

84   *The Ocean*

From *Childe Harold*, iv. 178.

There is a pleasure in the pathless woods,
There is a rapture on the lonely shore,
There is society, where none intrudes,
By the deep Sea, and music in its roar:

I love not Man the less, but Nature more,
From these our interviews, in which I steal
From all I may be, or have been before,
To mingle with the Universe, and feel
What I can ne'er express, yet cannot all conceal.

Roll on, thou deep and dark blue Ocean—roll !
Ten thousand fleets sweep over thee in vain ;
Man marks the earth with ruin—his control
Stops with the shore ;—upon the watery plain
The wrecks are all thy deed, nor doth remain
A shadow of man's ravage, save his own,
When, for a moment, like a drop of rain,
He sinks into thy depths with bubbling groan,
Without a grave, unknell'd, uncoffin'd, and unknown.

His steps are not upon thy paths,—thy fields
Are not a spoil for him,—thou dost arise
And shake him from thee ; the vile strength he wields
For earth's destruction thou dost all despise,
Spurning him from thy bosom to the skies,
And send'st him, shivering in thy playful spray
And howling, to his Gods, where haply lies
His petty hope in some near port or bay,
And dashest him again to earth :—there let him lay.

The armaments which thunderstrike the walls
Of rock-built cities, bidding nations quake
And monarchs tremble in their capitals,
The oak leviathans, whose huge ribs make
Their clay creator the vain title take
Of lord of thee, and arbiter of war ;
These are thy toys, and, as the snowy flake,
They melt into thy yeast of waves, which mar
Alike the Armada's pride or spoils of Trafalgar.

lay] lie, a vulgar solecism that invaded our public schools.

Thy shores are empires, changed in all save thee—
Assyria, Greece, Rome, Carthage, what are they ?
Thy waters wash'd them power while they were free,
And many a tyrant since ; their shores obey
The stranger, slave, or savage ; their decay
Has dried up realms to deserts :—not so thou—
Unchangeable save to thy wild waves' play—
Time writes no wrinkle on thine azure brow—
Such as creation's dawn beheld, thou rollest now.

Thou glorious mirror, where the Almighty's form
Glasses itself in tempests ; in all time,
Calm or convulsed—in breeze, or gale, or storm,
Icing the pole, or in the torrid clime
Dark-heaving ;—boundless, endless, and sublime—
The image of Eternity—the throne
Of the Invisible ; even from out thy slime
The monsters of the deep are made ; each zone
Obeys thee ; thou goest forth, dread, fathomless, alone.

And I have loved thee, Ocean ! and my joy
Of youthful sports was on thy breast to be
Borne, like thy bubbles, onward : from a boy
I wanton'd with thy breakers—they to me
Were a delight ; and if the freshening sea
Made them a terror—'twas a pleasing fear,
For I was as it were a child of thee,
And trusted to thy billows far and near,
And laid my hand upon thy mane—as I do here.

Byron.

85* *The Gleaming Sea*

WHEN winds that move not its calm surface sweep
The azure sea, I love the land no more ;
The smiles of the serene and tranquil deep
Tempt my unquiet mind.—But when the roar

Of Ocean's gray abyss resounds, and foam
Gathers upon the sea, and vast waves burst,
I turn from the drear aspect to the home
Of Earth and its deep woods, where, interspersed,
When winds blow loud, pines make sweet melody.
Whose house is some lone bark, whose toil the sea,
Whose prey the wandering fish, an evil lot
Has chosen.—But I my languid limbs will fling
Beneath the plane, where the brook's murmuring
Moves the calm spirit, but disturbs it not.

Shelley.

86　　　　　*The Sea*

It keeps eternal whisperings around
　Desolate shores, and with its mighty swell
　Gluts twice ten thousand Caverns, till the spell
Of Hecate leaves them their old shadowy sound.
Often 'tis in such gentle temper found,
　That scarcely will the very smallest shell
　Be moved for days from where it sometime fell,
When last the winds of Heaven were unbound.
Oh ye ! who have your eye-balls vex'd and tired,
　Feast them upon the wideness of the Sea ;
　　Oh ye ! whose ears are dinn'd with uproar rude,
Or fed too much with cloying melody—
　　Sit ye near some old Cavern's Mouth, and brood
Until ye start, as if the sea-nymphs quired !

Keats.

87　　　　*Prince Athanese*

'Twas at the season when the Earth upsprings
From slumber ; as a spherèd angel's child,
Shadowing its eyes with green and golden wings,
　Stands up before its mother bright and mild,

Of whose soft voice the air expectant seems—
So stood before the sun, which shone and smiled
   To see it rise thus joyous from its dreams,
The fresh and radiant Earth. The hoary grove
Wax'd green, and flowers burst forth like starry beams ;
   The grass in the warm sun did start and move,
And sea-buds burst under the waves serene.
How many a one, though none be near to love,
   Loves then the shade of his own soul, half seen
In any mirror—or the spring's young minions,
The wingèd leaves amid the copses green :
   How many a spirit then puts on the pinions
Of fancy, and outstrips the lagging blast,
And his own steps, and over wide dominions
   Sweeps in his dream-drawn chariot, far and fast,
More fleet than storms. The wide world shrinks below,
When winter and despondency are past. . . .

                         Shelley.

88   *To Meadows*

    Yᴇ have been fresh and green,
      Ye have been fill'd with flowers,
    And ye the walks have been
      Where maids have spent their hours.

    You have beheld how they
      With wicker arks did come
    To kiss and bear away
      The richer cowslips home.

    You 've heard them sweetly sing,
      And seen them in a round ;
    Each virgin like a spring,
      With honeysuckles crown'd.

        round] circular dance.

But now we see none here
   Whose silvery feet did tread
And with dishevell'd hair
   Adorn'd this smoother mead.

Like unthrifts, having spent
   Your stock and needy grown,
You 're left here to lament
   Your poor estates, alone.

                                      Herrick.

89*   *Hyperion*

I

DEEP in the shady sadness of a vale
Far sunken from the healthy breath of morn,
Far from the fiery noon, and eve's one star,
Sat gray-hair'd Saturn, quiet as a stone,
Still as the silence round about his lair ;
Forest on forest hung about his head
Like cloud on cloud.   No stir of air was there,
Not so much life as on a summer's day
Robs not one light seed from the feather'd grass,
But where the dead leaf fell, there did it rest.
A stream went voiceless by, still deaden'd more
By reason of his fallen divinity,
Spreading a shade : the Naiad 'mid her reeds
Press'd her cold finger closer to her lips.

   Along the margin-sand large foot-marks went,
No further than to where his feet had stray'd,
And slept there since.   Upon the sodden ground
His old right hand lay nerveless, listless, dead,
Unsceptred ; and his realmless eyes were closed ;
While his bow'd head seem'd list'ning to the Earth,
His ancient mother, for some comfort yet.

It seem'd no force could wake him from his place ;
But there came one, who with a kindred hand
Touch'd his wide shoulders, after bending low
With reverence, though to one who knew it not.
She was a Goddess of the infant world ;
By her in stature the tall Amazon
Had stood a pigmy's height : she would have ta'en
Achilles by the hair and bent his neck ;
Or with a finger stay'd Ixion's wheel.
Her face was large as that of Memphian sphinx,
Pedestal'd haply in a palace court,
When sages look'd to Egypt for their lore.
But oh ! how unlike marble was that face :
How beautiful, if sorrow had not made
Sorrow more beautiful than Beauty's self.
There was a listening fear in her regard,
As if calamity had but begun ;
As if the vanward clouds of evil days
Had spent their malice, and the sullen rear
Was with its storèd thunder labouring up.
One hand she press'd upon that aching spot
Where beats the human heart, as if just there,
Though an immortal, she felt cruel pain :
The other upon Saturn's bended neck
She laid, and to the level of his ear
Leaning with parted lips, some words she spake
In solemn tenour and deep organ tone :
Some mourning words, which in our feeble tongue
Would come in these-like accents ; O how frail
To that large utterance of the early Gods ! . . .

II

As when, upon a trancèd summer-night,
Those green-robed senators of mighty woods,
Tall oaks, branch-charmèd by the earnest stars,
Dream, and so dream all night without a stir,

Save from one gradual solitary gust
Which comes upon the silence, and dies off,
As if the ebbing air had but one wave ;
So came these words and went ; the while in tears
She touch'd her fair large forehead to the ground,
Just where her falling hair might be outspread
A soft and silken mat for Saturn's feet.
One moon, with alteration slow, had shed
Her silver seasons four upon the night,
And still these two were postured motionless,
Like natural sculpture in cathedral cavern ;
The frozen God still couchant on the earth,
And the sad Goddess weeping at his feet :
Until at length old Saturn lifted up
His faded eyes, and saw his kingdom gone,
And all the gloom and sorrow of the place,
And that fair kneeling Goddess. . . .

Keats.

90   *The Willow*

Leans now the fair willow, dreaming
Amid her locks of green.
In the driving snow she was parch'd and cold,
And in midnight hath been
Swept by blasts of the void night,
Lash'd by the rains.
Now of that wintry dark and bleak
No memory remains.

In mute desire she sways softly ;
Thrilling sap up-flows ;
She praises God in her beauty and grace,
Whispers delight. And there flows

A delicate wind from the Southern seas,
Kissing her leaves.   She sighs.
While the birds in her tresses make merry ;
Burns the Sun in the skies.

Walter de la Mare.

91   *Song*

The feathers of the willow
Are half of them grown yellow
    Above the swelling stream ;
And ragged are the bushes,
And rusty now the rushes,
    And wild the clouded gleam.

The thistle now is older,
His stalk begins to moulder,
    His head is white as snow ;
The branches all are barer,
The linnet's song is rarer,
    The robin pipeth now.

Dixon

92

I

A SPIRIT haunts the year's last hours
Dwelling amid these yellowing bowers:
    To himself he talks ;
For at eventide, listening earnestly,
At his work you may hear him sob and sigh
    In the walks ;
    Earthward he boweth the heavy stalks
Of the mouldering flowers :
    Heavily hangs the broad sunflower
        Over its grave i' the earth so chilly ;
    Heavily hangs the hollyhock,
        Heavily hangs the tiger-lily.

II

The air is damp, and hush'd, and close,
As a sick man's room when he taketh repose
    An hour before death ;
My very heart faints and my whole soul grieves
At the moist rich smell of the rotting leaves,
        And the breath
        Of the fading edges of box beneath,
And the year's last rose.
        Heavily hangs the broad sunflower
            Over its grave i' the earth so chilly ;
        Heavily hangs the hollyhock,
            Heavily hangs the tiger-lily.

                                        Tennyson.

93   *Ode to Autumn*

I

SEASON of mists and mellow fruitfulness,
    Close bosom-friend of the maturing sun ;
Conspiring with him how to load and bless
    With fruit the vines that round the thatch-eaves run ;
To bend with apples the moss'd cottage-trees,
    And fill all fruit with ripeness to the core ;
        To swell the gourd, and plump the hazel shells
    With a sweet kernel ; to set budding more,
And still more, later flowers for the bees,
Until they think warm days will never cease,
        For Summer has o'er-brimm'd their clammy cells.

II

Who hath not seen thee oft amid thy store ?
    Sometimes whoever seeks abroad may find
Thee sitting careless on a granary floor,
    Thy hair soft-lifted by the winnowing wind ;

Or on a half-reap'd furrow sound asleep,
  Drowsed with the fume of poppies, while thy hook
    Spares the next swath and all its twinèd flowers :
And sometime like a gleaner thou dost keep
  Steady thy laden head across a brook ;
  Or by a cider-press, with patient look,
    Thou watchest the last oozings hours by hours.

III

Where are the songs of Spring ? Ay, where are they ?
  Think not of them, thou hast thy music too,—
While barrèd clouds bloom the soft-dying day,
  And touch the stubble-plains with rosy hue ;
Then in a wailful choir the small gnats mourn
  Among the river sallows, borne aloft
    Or sinking as the light wind lives or dies ;
And full-grown lambs loud bleat from hilly bourn ;
  Hedge-crickets sing ; and now with treble soft
  The redbreast whistles from a garden-croft ;
    And gathering swallows twitter in the skies.

                                   Keats.

94   *Hymn to Diana*

QUEEN and huntress, chaste and fair,
  Now the sun is laid to sleep,
Seated in thy silver chair,
  State in wonted manner keep :
    Hesperus entreats thy light,
    Goddess excellently bright.

Earth, let not thy envious shade
  Dare itself to interpose ;
Cynthia's shining orb was made
  Heaven to clear when day did close :
    Bless us then with wishèd sight,
    Goddess excellently bright.

Lay thy bow of pearl apart,
　And thy crystal-shining quiver ;
Give unto the flying hart
　Space to breathe, how short soever :
　　Thou that mak'st a day of night—
　　Goddess excellently bright.

Ben Jonson.

95　　　　*The Waning Moon*

AND like a dying lady, lean and pale,
Who totters forth, wrapp'd in a gauzy veil,
Out of her chamber, led by the insane
And feeble wanderings of her fading brain,
The moon arose up in the murky East,
A white and shapeless mass—

Shelley.

96*

. . . How sweet the moonlight sleeps upon this bank !
Here will we sit and let the sounds of music
Creep in our ears : soft stillness and the night
Become the touches of sweet harmony.
Sit, Jessica.　Look how the floor of heaven
Is thick inlaid with patines of bright gold :
There 's not the smallest orb which thou behold'st
But in his motion like an angel sings,
Still quiring to the young-eyed cherubins ;
Such harmony is in immortal souls ;
But whilst this muddy vesture of decay
Doth grossly close it in, we cannot hear it. . . .

Shakespeare.

patines] paten (pronounced patten), the Eucharistic dish, hence
any small flat circular plate of gold.

97   *Westminster Bridge*

EARTH has not anything to show more fair :
Dull would he be of soul who could pass by
A sight so touching in its majesty :
This City now doth, like a garment, wear
The beauty of the morning ; silent, bare,
Ships, towers, domes, theatres, and temples lie
Open unto the fields, and to the sky ;
All bright and glittering in the smokeless air.

Never did sun more beautifully steep
In his first splendour, valley, rock, or hill ;
Ne'er saw I, never felt, a calm so deep !
The river glideth at his own sweet will :
Dear God ! the very houses seem asleep ;
And all that mighty heart is lying still !

                                    Wordsworth, 1802.

98

As through the wild green hills of Wyre
The train ran, changing sky and shire,
And far behind, a fading crest,
Low in the forsaken west
Sank the high-rear'd head of Clee,
My hand lay empty on my knee.
Aching on my knee it lay :
That morning half a shire away
So many an honest fellow's fist
Had well-nigh wrung it from the wrist.
Hand, said I, since now we part
From fields and men we know by heart,
For strangers' faces, strangers' lands,—
Hand, you have held true fellows' hands.

                    H

Be clean then ; rot before you do
A thing they 'd not believe of you.
You and I must keep from shame
In London streets the Shropshire name ;
On banks of Thames they must not say
Severn breeds worse men than they ;
And friends abroad must bear in mind
Friends at home they leave behind.
Oh, I shall be stiff and cold
When I forget you, hearts of gold ;
The land where I shall mind you not
Is the land where all 's forgot.
And if my foot returns no more
To Teme nor Corve nor Severn shore,
Luck, my lads, be with you still
By falling stream and standing hill,
By chiming tower and whispering tree
Men that made a man of me.
About your work in town and farm
Still you 'll keep my head from harm,
Still you 'll help me, hands that gave
A grasp to friend me to the grave.

A. E. Housman.

99   *Song in Absence*

GREEN fields of England ! wheresoe'er
Across this watery waste we fare,
Your image at our hearts we bear,
Green fields of England, everywhere.

Sweet eyes in England, I must flee
Past where the waves' last confines be,
Ere your loved smile I cease to see,
Sweet eyes in England, dear to me !

Dear home in England, safe and fast
If but in thee my lot lie cast,
The past shall seem a nothing past
To thee, dear home, if won at last ;
Dear home in England, won at last.

Clough, 1852.

100   *Home-Thoughts from Abroad*

OH, to be in England
Now that April 's there,
And whoever wakes in England
Sees, some morning, unaware,
That the lowest boughs and the brushwood sheaf
Round the elm-tree bole are in tiny leaf,
While the chaffinch sings on the orchard bough
        In England—now !

   And after April, when May follows,
And the whitethroat builds, and all the swallows !
Hark, where my blossom'd pear-tree in the hedge
Leans to the field and scatters on the clover
Blossoms and dewdrops—at the bent spray's edge—
That 's the wise thrush ; he sings each song twice over,
Lest you should think he never could recapture
The first fine careless rapture !
And though the fields look rough with hoary dew,
All will be gay when noontide wakes anew
The buttercups, the little children's dower
—Far brighter than this gaudy melon-flower !

Browning.

101   *The Soldier's Dream*

OUR bugles sang truce—for the night-cloud had lower'd,
   And the sentinel stars set their watch in the sky ;
And thousands had sunk on the ground overpower'd,
   The weary to sleep, and the wounded to die.

When reposing that night on my pallet of straw,
    By the wolf-scaring faggot that guarded the slain,
At the dead of the night a sweet vision I saw,
    And thrice ere the morning I dreamt it again.

Methought from the battle-field's dreadful array,
    Far, far I had roam'd on a desolate track :
'Twas autumn,—and sunshine arose on the way
    To the home of my fathers, that welcomed me back.

I flew to the pleasant fields traversed so oft
    In life's morning march, when my bosom was young;
I heard my own mountain-goats bleating aloft,
    And knew the sweet strain that the corn-reapers
        sung.

Then pledged we the wine-cup, and fondly I swore,
    From my home and my weeping friends never to part;
My little ones kiss'd me a thousand times o'er,
    And my wife sobb'd aloud in her fulness of heart.

' Stay, stay with us !—rest ! thou art weary and worn ' ;
    And fain was their war-broken soldier to stay ;—
But sorrow return'd with the dawning of morn,
    And the voice in my dreaming ear—melted away.
                                        Campbell.

102   *Vailima*

BLOWS the wind to-day, and the sun and the rain are
        flying,
    Blows the wind on the moors to-day and now,
Where about the graves of the martyrs the whaups are
        crying,
    My heart remembers how !

> Blows] inversion of grammar = the wind blows.
> whaups] curlews.

Grey recumbent tombs of the dead in desert places,
  Standing-stones on the vacant wine-red moor,
Hills of sheep, and the homes of the silent vanish'd
    races,
  And winds, austere and pure :

Be it granted me to behold you again in dying,
  Hills of home ! and to hear again the call ;
Hear about the graves of the martyrs the peewees
    crying,
  And hear no more at all.

Stevenson.

103 *Gaunt's Dying Speech*

From *Richard II.* ii. i.

GAUNT. Will the king come, that I may breathe my
    last
In wholesome counsel to his unstaid youth ?
  YORK. Vex not yourself, nor strive not with your
    breath ;
For all in vain comes counsel to his ear.
  GAUNT. Oh, but they say the tongues of dying men
Enforce attention like deep harmony :
Where words are scarce, they are seldom spent in vain,
For they breathe truth that breathe their words in pain.
He that no more must say is listen'd more
Than they whom youth and ease have taught to glose ;
More are men's ends mark'd than their lives before :
The setting sun, and music at the close,
As the last taste of sweets is sweetest, last,
Writ in remembrance more than things long past :
Though Richard my life's counsel would not hear,
My death's sad tale may yet undeaf his ear.
  YORK. No ; it is stopp'd with other flattering
    sounds, . . .

Direct not him whose way himself will choose :
'Tis breath thou lack'st, and that breath wilt thou lose.

GAUNT. Methinks I am a prophet new inspired
And thus expiring do foretell of him :
His rash fierce blaze of riot cannot last,
For violent fires soon burn out themselves ;
Small showers last long, but sudden storms are short ;
He tires betimes that spurs too fast betimes ;
With eager feeding food doth choke the feeder :
Light vanity, insatiate cormorant,
Consuming means, soon preys upon itself.
This royal throne of kings, this sceptred isle,
This earth of majesty, this seat of Mars,
This other Eden, demi-paradise,
This fortress built by Nature for herself
Against infection and the hand of war,
This happy breed of men, this little world,
This precious stone set in the silver sea,
Which serves it in the office of a wall
Or as a moat defensive to a house,
Against the envy of less happier lands,
This blessed plot, this earth, this realm, this England,
This nurse, this teeming womb of royal kings,
Fear'd by their breed and famous by their birth,
Renownèd for their deeds as far from home,
For Christian service and true chivalry,
As is the sepulchre in stubborn Jewry
Of the world's ransom, blessed Mary's Son,
This land of such dear souls, this dear dear land,
Dear for her reputation through the world,
Is now leased out, I die pronouncing it,
Like to a tenement or pelting farm :
England, bound in with the triumphant sea,
Whose rocky shore beats back the envious siege
Of watery Neptune, is now bound in with shame,

pelting] paltry, petty.

With inky blots and rotten parchment bonds :
That England, that was wont to conquer others,
Hath made a shameful conquest of itself.
Ah, would the scandal vanish with my life,
How happy then were my ensuing death ! . . .

Shakespeare.

104   *London,* 1802

MILTON ! thou shouldst be living at this hour :
England hath need of thee : she is a fen
Of stagnant waters : altar, sword, and pen,
Fireside, the heroic wealth of hall and bower,
Have forfeited their ancient English dower
Of inward happiness.   We are selfish men ;
Oh ! raise us up, return to us again ;
And give us manners, virtue, freedom, power.

Thy soul was like a Star, and dwelt apart ;
Thou hadst a voice whose sound was like the sea :
Pure as the naked heavens, majestic, free,
So didst thou travel on life's common way,
In cheerful godliness ; and yet thy heart
The lowliest duties on herself did lay.

Wordsworth.

105

   BREATHES there the man with soul so dead,
   Who never to himself hath said,
     ' This is my own, my native land ! '
   Whose heart hath ne'er within him burn'd,
   As home his footsteps he hath turn'd,
     From wandering on a foreign strand ?
   If such there breathe, go, mark him well ;
   For him no minstrel raptures swell ;

High though his titles, proud his name,
Boundless his wealth as wish can claim ;
Despite those titles, power, and pelf,
The wretch, concentred all in self,
Living, shall forfeit fair renown,
And, doubly dying, shall go down
To the vile dust, from whence he sprung,
Unwept, unhonour'd, and unsung.

O Caledonia ! stern and wild,
Meet nurse for a poetic child !
Land of brown heath and shaggy wood,
Land of the mountain and the flood,
Land of my sires ! what mortal hand
Can e'er untie the filial band
That knits me to thy rugged strand ! . . .

*Scott.**

106*   *Epitaph on a Jacobite*

To my true king I offer'd free from stain
Courage and faith ; vain faith, and courage vain.
For him, I threw lands, honours, wealth, away,
And one dear hope, that was more prized than they.
For him I languish'd in a foreign clime,
Grey-hair'd with sorrow in my manhood's prime ;
Heard on Lavernia Scargill's whispering trees,
And pined by Arno for my lovelier Tees ;
Beheld each night my home in fever'd sleep,
Each morning started from the dream to weep ;
Till God, who saw me tried too sorely, gave
The resting-place I ask'd, an early grave.
O thou, whom chance leads to this nameless stone,
From that proud country which was once mine own,

concentred] pronounce concenter'd.

By those white cliffs I never more must see,
By that dear language which I spake like thee,
Forget all feuds, and shed one English tear
O'er English dust.   A broken heart lies here.

Macaulay.

107   *Bolingbroke (afterwards Henry IV.), having
heard from the King his sentence of ban-
ishment for six years, stands silent.   His
father, John of Gaunt, would comfort
him.*

From *Richard II.* i. iii.

. . . GAUNT. Oh, to what purpose dost thou hoard
   thy words,
That thou return'st no greeting to thy friends ?
   BOLING. I have too few to take my leave of you.
When the tongue's office should be prodigal
To breathe the abundant dolour of the heart.
   GAUNT. Thy grief is but thy absence for a time.
   BOLING. Joy absent, grief is present for that time.
   GAUNT. What is six winters ? they are quickly gone.
   BOLING. To men in joy ; but grief makes one hour ten.
   GAUNT. Call it a travel that thou takest for pleasure.
   BOLING. My heart will sigh when I miscall it so,
Which finds it an inforcèd pilgrimage.
   GAUNT. The sullen passage of thy weary steps
Esteem a foil wherein thou art to set
The precious jewel of thy home return.
   BOLING. Nay, rather, every tedious stride I make
Will but remember me what a deal of world
I wander from the jewels that I love.
Must I not serve a long apprenticehood
To foreign passages, and in the end,

Having my freedom, boast of nothing else
But that I was a journeyman to grief ?

GAUNT. All places that the eye of heaven visits
Are to a wise man ports and happy havens.
Teach thy necessity to reason thus ;
There is no virtue like necessity.
Think not the king did banish thee,
But thou the king.   Woe doth the heavier sit,
Where it perceives it is but faintly borne.
Go say I sent thee forth to purchase honour
And not the king exiled thee ; or suppose
Devouring pestilence hangs in our air
And thou art flying to a fresher clime :
Look, what thy soul holds dear, imagine it
To lie that way thou go'st, not whence thou comest :
Suppose the singing birds musicians,
The grass whereon thou tread'st the presence strew'd,
The flowers fair ladies, and thy steps no more
Than a delightful measure or a dance ;
For gnarling sorrow hath less power to bite
The man that mocks at it and sets it light.

BOLING. Oh, who can hold a fire in his hand
By thinking on the frosty Caucasus ?
Or cloy the hungry edge of appetite
By bare imagination of a feast ?
Or wallow naked in December snow
By thinking on fantastic summer's heat ?
Oh, no ! the apprehension of the good
Gives but the greater feeling to the worse :
Fell sorrow's tooth doth never rankle more
Than when he bites, but lanceth not the sore.

GAUNT. Come, come, my son, I 'll bring thee on thy way:
Had I thy youth and cause, I would not stay.

journeyman] one who has served his *apprenticeship* and may work
under a *master* for hire.   There is a play here on the word *journey* =
travel.

Boling. Then, England's ground, farewell; sweet
    soil, adieu;
My mother, and my nurse, that bears me yet!
Where'er I wander, boast of this I can,
Though banish'd, yet a trueborn Englishman.

Shakespeare.

108

A THING of beauty is a joy for ever:
Its loveliness increases; it will never
Pass into nothingness; but still will keep
A bower quiet for us, and a sleep
Full of sweet dreams, and health, and quiet breathing.
Therefore, on every morrow, are we wreathing
A flowery band to bind us to the earth,
Spite of despondence, of the inhuman dearth
Of noble natures, of the gloomy days,
Of all the unhealthy and o'er-darken'd ways
Made for our searching: yes, in spite of all,
Some shape of beauty moves away the pall
From our dark spirits. Such the sun, the moon,
Trees old and young, sprouting a shady boon
For simple sheep; and such are daffodils
With the green world they live in; and clear rills
That for themselves a cooling covert make
'Gainst the hot season; the mid-forest brake,
Rich with a sprinkling of fair musk-rose blooms:
And such too is the grandeur of the dooms
We have imagined for the mighty dead;
All lovely tales that we have heard or read:
An endless fountain of immortal drink,
Pouring unto us from the heaven's brink.

Nor do we merely feel these essences
For one short hour; no, even as the trees

That whisper round a temple become soon
Dear as the temple's self, so does the moon,
The passion poesy, glories infinite,
Haunt us till they become a cheering light
Unto our souls, and bound to us so fast,
That, whether there be shine, or gloom o'ercast,
They alway must be with us, or we die. . . .

*Keats.**

109 *Spirit's Song in ' Prometheus '*

ON a poet's lips I slept
Dreaming like a love-adept
In the sound his breathing kept ;
Nor seeks nor finds he mortal blisses,
But feeds on the aëral kisses
Of shapes that haunt thought's wildernesses.
He will watch from dawn to gloom
The lake-reflected sun illume
The yellow bees in the ivy-bloom,
Nor heed nor see, what things they be ;
But from these create he can
Forms more real than living man,
Nurslings of immortality !
One of these awaken'd me,
And I sped to succour thee.

Shelley.

110* *The Immortal Muse*

. . . Thou art light and thou art free,
And to live rejoiceth thee,
Where the splendours greatest be. . . .

adept] one completely skilled in all the secrets of his art.

Thou a seraph art to go
All undaunted to and fro
Where the fiercest ardours glow. . . .

Thou an angel art, and well
It sufficeth thee to dwell
In the smallest creature's cell. . . .

Thou a spirit art most sweet,
And to make all life complete
Everywhere thou hast thy seat.

Dixon.

III   *The Question*

I

I DREAM'D that, as I wander'd by the way,
  Bare Winter suddenly was changed to Spring,
And gentle odours led my steps astray,
  Mix'd with a sound of waters murmuring
Along a shelving bank of turf, which lay
  Under a copse, and hardly dared to fling
Its green arms round the bosom of the stream,
But kiss'd it and then fled, as thou mightest in dream.

II

There grew pied wind-flowers and violets,
  Daisies, those pearl'd Arcturi of the earth,
The constellated flower that never sets ;
  Faint oxslips ; tender bluebells, at whose birth
The sod scarce heaved ; and that tall flower that wets—
  Like a child, half in tenderness and mirth—
Its mother's face with Heaven's collected tears,
When the low wind, its playmate's voice, it hears.

Arcturi] northern stars.
that tall flower] the ' Crown Imperial ' (?).

III

And in the warm hedge grew lush eglantine,
  Green cowbind and the moonlight-colour'd may,
And cherry-blossoms, and white cups, whose wine
  Was the bright dew, yet drain'd not by the day ;
And wild roses, and ivy serpentine,
  With its dark buds and leaves, wandering astray ;
And flowers azure, black, and streak'd with gold,
Fairer than any waken'd eyes behold.

IV

And nearer to the river's trembling edge
  There grew broad flag-flowers, purple prank'd with
    white,
And starry river-buds among the sedge,
  And floating water-lilies, broad and bright,
Which lit the oak that overhung the hedge
  With moonlight beams of their own watery light ;
And bulrushes, and reeds of such deep green
As soothed the dazzled eye with sober sheen.

V

Methought that of these visionary flowers
  I made a nosegay, bound in such a way
That the same hues which in their natural bowers
  Were mingled or opposed, the like array
Kept these imprison'd children of the Hours
  Within my hand—and then, elate and gay,
I hasten'd to the spot whence I had come,
That I might there present it !—Oh, to whom ?

Shelley.

eglantine] sweet-briar.   cowbind] Bryony.

112   *To Helen*

HELEN, thy beauty is to me
　　Like those Nicéan barks of yore
That gently, o'er a perfumed sea,
　　The weary way-worn wanderer bore
　　To his own native shore.

On desperate seas long wont to roam,
　　Thy hyacinth hair, thy classic face,
Thy Naiad airs have brought me home
　　To the glory that was Greece,
　　And the grandeur that was Rome.

Lo ! in yon brilliant window-niche
　　How statue-like I see thee stand,
　　The agate lamp within thy hand,—
Ah ! Psyche, from the regions which
　　Are Holy Land !

　　　　　　　　　　　　　　Poe.

113

THERE be none of Beauty's daughters
　　With a magic like thee ;
And like music on the waters
　　Is thy sweet voice to me :
When, as if its sound were causing
The charmed ocean's pausing,
The waves lie still and gleaming,
And the lull'd winds seem dreaming.

And the midnight moon is weaving
　　Her bright chain o'er the deep ;
Whose breast is gently heaving,
　　As an infant's asleep :

So the spirit bows before thee,
To listen and adore thee ;
With a full but soft emotion,
Like the swell of Summer's ocean.

Byron.

114 *The Solitary Reaper*

BEHOLD her, single in the field,
Yon solitary Highland Lass !
Reaping and singing by herself ;
Stop here, or gently pass !
Alone she cuts and binds the grain,
And sings a melancholy strain ;
O listen ! for the Vale profound
Is overflowing with the sound.

No Nightingale did ever chaunt
More welcome notes to weary bands
Of travellers in some shady haunt,
Among Arabian sands :
A voice so thrilling ne'er was heard
In spring-time from the Cuckoo-bird,
Breaking the silence of the seas
Among the farthest Hebrides.

Will no one tell me what she sings ?—
Perhaps the plaintive numbers flow
For old, unhappy, far-off things,
And battles long ago :
Or is it some more humble lay,
Familiar matter of to-day ?
Some natural sorrow, loss, or pain.
That has been, and may be again ? . . .

Whate'er the theme, the Maiden sang
As if her song could have no ending ;
I saw her singing at her work,
And o'er the sickle bending ;
I listen'd, motionless and still ;
And, when I mounted up the hill,
The music in my heart I bore,
Long after it was heard no more.

Wordsworth, 1804.

115 *Ferry Hinksey*

Beyond the ferry water
That fast and silent flow'd,
She turn'd, she gazed a moment,
Then took her onward road

Between the winding willows
To a city white with spires :
It seem'd a path of pilgrims
To the home of earth's desires.

Blue shade of golden branches
Spread for her journeying,
Till he that linger'd lost her
Among the leaves of Spring.

Laurence Binyon.

116 *The Wayfarer*

Keen, fitful gusts are whisp'ring here and there
Among the bushes, half leafless and dry ;
The stars look very cold about the sky,
And I have many miles on foot to fare.

I

Yet feel I little of the cool bleak air,
  Or of the dead leaves rustling drearily,
  Or of those silver lamps that burn on high,
Or of the distance from home's pleasant lair :
For I am brimfull of the friendliness
  That in a little cottage I have found ;
Of fair-hair'd Milton's eloquent distress,
  And all his love for gentle Lycid drown'd ;
Of lovely Laura in her light green dress,
  And faithful Petrarch gloriously crown'd.

Keats

117   *On the Sea-Shore*

It is a beauteous evening, calm and free,
  The holy time is quiet as a Nun
  Breathless with adoration ; the broad sun
Is sinking down in its tranquillity ;

The gentleness of heaven broods o'er the Sea :
  Listen ! the mighty Being is awake,
  And doth with his eternal motion make
A sound like thunder—everlastingly.

Dear Child ! dear Girl ! that walkest with me here,
  If thou appear untouch'd by solemn thought,
  Thy nature is not therefore less divine :

Thou liest in Abraham's bosom all the year,
    And worshipp'st at the Temple's inner shrine,
God being with thee when we know it not.

Wordsworth, 1802.

118

IT was a lover and his lass,
  With a hey, and a ho, and a hey nonino !
That o'er the green corn-field did pass
  In the Spring time, the only pretty ring time,
When birds do sing, hey ding a ding, ding ;
    Sweet lovers love the Spring.

Between the acres of the rye,
  With a hey, and a ho, and a hey nonino !
These pretty country folks would lie,
  In Spring time, etc.

This carol they began that hour,
  With a hey, and a ho, and a hey nonino !
How that life was but a flower
  In Spring time, etc.

And therefore take the present time,
  With a hey, and a ho, and a hey nonino !
For love is crownèd with the prime
  In Spring time, the only pretty ring time,
When birds do sing, hey ding a ding, ding ;
    Sweet lovers love the Spring.

                                    Shakespeare.

119   *Madrigal*

        FAIN would I change that note
        To which fond Love hath charm'd me
        Long, long to sing by rote,
        Fancying that that harm'd me :

  that that] accent on the first *that*, viz. : liking (all the while) that
which harmed me.

Yet when this thought doth come,
' Love is the perfect sum
   Of all delight,'
I have no other choice
Either for pen or voice
   To sing or write.

O Love ! they wrong thee much
That say thy sweet is bitter,
When thy rich fruit is such
As nothing can be sweeter.
Fair house of joy and bliss,
Where truest pleasure is,
   I do adore thee :
I know thee what thou art,
I serve thee with my heart,
   And fall before thee.

1605.

120

I KNOW not what my secret is,
   I know but it is mine,
I know to dwell with it were bliss,
   To die for it divine.

I cannot yield it in a kiss,
   Nor breathe it in a sigh ;
Enough that I have lived for this,
   For this, my love, I die.

Lang.

121*   *The Bargain*

My true Love hath my heart, and I have his,
   By just exchange one for the other given :
I hold his dear, and mine he cannot miss ;
   There never was a better bargain driven.

His heart in me keeps me and him in one,
  My heart in him his thoughts and senses guides :
He loves my heart, for once it was his own ;
  I cherish his, because in me it bides . . .
    My true Love hath my heart, and I have his.
                                          Sidney.

122* *To Althea from Prison*

>   Stone walls do not a prison make,
>   Nor iron bars a cage ;
>   Minds innocent and quiet take
>   That for a hermitage :
>   If I have freedom in my love
>   And in my soul am free,
>   Angels alone, that soar above,
>   Enjoy such liberty.
>   *Lovelace.*

123

Oh, talk not to me of a name great in story ,
The days of our youth are the days of our glory ;
And the myrtle and ivy of sweet two-and-twenty
Are worth all your laurels, tho' ever so plenty.

What are garlands and crowns to the brow that is
    wrinkled ?
'Tis but as a dead-flower with May-dew besprinkled—
Then away with all such from the head that is hoary !
What care I for the wreaths that can only give glory ?

O Fame !—If I e'er took delight in thy praises,
'Twas less for the sake of thy high sounding phrases,
Than to see the bright eyes of the dear one discover
She thought that I was not unworthy to love her.

    high sounding] high-sounding is probably intended.

There chiefly I sought thee, there only I found thee ;
Her glance was the best of the rays that surround thee ;
When it sparkled o'er aught that was bright in my story,
I knew it was love, and I felt it was glory.

Byron, 1821.

124   *Lucy*

SHE dwelt among the untrodden ways
  Beside the springs of Dove,
A Maid whom there were none to praise
  And very few to love :

A violet by a mossy stone
  Half hidden from the eye !
Fair as a star, when only one
  Is shining in the sky.

She lived unknown, and few could know
  When Lucy ceased to be ;
But she is in her grave, and, oh,
  The difference to me !

Wordsworth, 1799.

125

O snatch'd away in beauty's bloom,
On thee shall press no ponderous tomb ;
But on thy turf shall roses rear
Their leaves, the earliest of the year ;
And the wild cypress wave in tender gloom :

And oft by yon blue gushing stream
Shall Sorrow lean her drooping head,
And feed deep thought with many a dream,
And lingering pause and lightly tread ;
Fond wretch ! as if her steps disturb'd the dead !

Away ! We know that tears are vain,
That death nor heeds nor hears distress :
Will this unteach us to complain,
Or make one mourner weep the less ?
And thou—who tell'st me to forget,
Thy looks are wan, thine eyes are wet.

Byron, 1815.

126

I

WHEN the lamp is shatter'd
The light in the dust lies dead—
  When the cloud is scatter'd
The rainbow's glory is shed.
  When the lute is broken,
Sweet tones are remember'd not ;
  When the lips have spoken,
Loved accents are soon forgot.

II

  As music and splendour
Survive not the lamp and the lute,
  The heart's echoes render
No song when the spirit is mute :—
  No song but sad dirges,
Like the wind through a ruin'd cell,
  Or the mournful surges
That ring the dead seaman's knell.

III

  When hearts have once mingled
Love first leaves the well-built nest ;
  The weak one is singled
To endure what it once possess'd.

O Love ! who bewailest
The frailty of all things here,
   Why choose you the frailest
For your cradle, your home, and your bier ?

IV

   Its passions will rock thee
As the storms rock the ravens on high ;
   Bright reason will mock thee,
Like the sun from a wintry sky.
   From thy nest every rafter
Will rot, and thine eagle home
   Leave thee naked to laughter,
When leaves fall and cold winds come.

Shelley.

127

My silks and fine array,
   My smiles and languish'd air,
By love are driven away :
   And mournful lean Despair
Brings me yew to deck my grave :
Such end true lovers have.

His face is fair as heaven
   When springing buds unfold ;
O why to him was 't given
   Whose heart is wintry cold ?
His breast is love's all-worship'd tomb,
Where all love's pilgrims come.

Bring me an axe and spade,
   Bring me a winding sheet ;
When I my grave have made,
   Let winds and tempests beat :
Then down I 'll lie, as cold as clay.
True love doth pass away !

Blake.

128

THE night has a thousand eyes,
    And the day but one ;
Yet the light of the bright world dies
    With the dying sun.

The mind has a thousand eyes,
    And the heart but one ;
Yet the light of a whole life dies,
    When love is done.

Bourdillon.

129

Away ! The moor is dark beneath the moon,
    Rapid clouds have drank the last pale beam of even :
Away ! the gathering winds will call the darkness
        soon,
    And profoundest midnight shroud the sérene lights
        of heaven.

Pause not ! The time is past ! Every voice cries, Away !
    Tempt not with one last tear thy friend's ungentle
        mood :
Thy lover's eye, so glazed and cold, dares not entreat
        thy stay,
    Duty and dereliction guide thee back to solitude.

Away, away ! to thy sad and silent home ;
    Pour bitter tears on its desolated hearth ;
Watch the dim shades as like ghosts they go and come,
    And complicate strange webs of melancholy mirth.

                    sérene]*.

The leaves of wasted autumn woods shall float around
    thine head :
  The blooms of dewy spring shall gleam beneath thy
    feet :
But thy soul or this world must fade in the frost that
    binds the dead,
  Ere midnight's frown and morning's smile, ere thou
    and peace may meet.

The cloud shadows of midnight possess their own repose,
  For the weary winds are silent, or the moon is in the
    deep :
Some respite to its turbulence unresting ocean knows ;
  Whatever moves, or toils, or grieves, hath its ap-
    pointed sleep.

Thou in the grave shalt rest—yet till the phantoms flee
  Which that house and heath and garden made dear
    to thee erewhile,
Thy remembrance, and repentance, and deep musings
    are not free
  From the music of two voices and the light of one
    sweet smile.

Shelley.

130*   *Lycidas*

In this Monody the Author bewails a learned Friend,
unfortunately drown'd in his Passage from *Chester* on the
Irish Seas, 1637. And by occasion foretels the ruine of
our corrupted clergy then in their height.

    YET once more, O ye Laurels, and once more
    Ye Myrtles brown, with Ivy never-sere,
    I come to pluck your Berries harsh and crude,
    And, with forced fingers rude,
    Shatter your leaves before the mellowing year

Bitter constraint, and sad occasion dear,
Compels me to disturb your season due :
For *Lycidas* is dead, dead ere his prime,
Young *Lycidas*, and hath not left his peer :
Who would not sing for *Lycidas* ? he knew   10
Himself to sing, and build the lofty rhyme.
He must not float upon his watery bier
Unwept, and welter to the parching wind,
Without the meed of some melodious tear.

  Begin then, Sisters of the sacred well,
That from beneath the seat of *Jove* doth spring,
Begin, and somewhat loudly sweep the string :
Hence with denial vain, and coy excuse ;
So may some gentle Muse
With lucky words favour my destined Urn,   20
And as he passes turn,
And bid fair peace be to my sable shroud.

  For we were nursed upon the self-same hill,
Fed the same flock, by fountain, shade, and rill.
Together both, ere the high Lawns appear'd
Under the opening eye-lids of the morn,
We drove a-field, and both together heard
What time the Gray-fly winds her sultry horn,
Battening our flocks with the fresh dews of night ;
Oft till the Star that rose, at Evening, bright   30
Toward Heav'n's descent had sloped his westering wheel.
Meanwhile the rural ditties were not mute,
Temper'd to th' oaten Flute ;
Rough *Satyrs* danced, and *Fauns* with cloven heel
From the glad sound would not be absent long,
And old *Damœtas* loved to hear our song.

  But O the heavy change, now thou art gone,
Now thou art gone, and never must return !
Thee, Shepherd, thee the Woods, and desert Caves

rhyme] verse.   sacred well] Helicon.
hill] *.   oaten] shepherd's pipe.

With wild Thyme and the gadding Vine o'ergrown,   40
And all their echoes mourn.
The Willows and the Hazle-Copses green
Shall now no more be seen
Fanning their joyous Leaves to thy soft lays.
As killing as the Canker to the Rose,
Or Taint-worm to the weanling Herds that graze,
Or Frost to Flowers, that their gay wardrobe wear,
When first the White-thorn blows ;
Such, *Lycidas*, thy loss to Shepherds' ear.

Where were ye Nymphs when the remorseless deep
Closed o'er the head of your loved *Lycidas* ?   51
For neither were ye playing on the steep,
Where your old *Bards*, the famous *Druids* lie,
Nor on the shaggy top of *Mona* high,
Nor yet where *Deva* spreads her wizard stream :
Ay me, I fondly dream!
Had ye bin there—for what could that have done ?
What could the Muse herself that *Orpheus* bore,
The Muse herself, for her enchanting son
Whom universal nature did lament,   60
When by the rout that made the hideous roar,
His gory visage down the stream was sent,
Down the swift *Hebrus* to the *Lesbian* shore ?

Alas ! What boots it with incessant care
To tend the homely slighted Shepherd's trade,
And strictly meditate the thankless Muse ?
Were it not better done as others use,
To sport with *Amaryllis* in the shade,
Or with the tangles of *Neæra's* hair ?
Fame is the spur that the clear spirit doth raise   70
(That last infirmity of noble mind)
To scorn delights, and live laborious days ;
But the fair Guerdon when we hope to find,
And think to burst out into sudden blaze,

boots] avails.

Comes the blind *Fury* with the abhorrèd shears,
And slits the thin-spun life. ' But not the praise,'
Phœbus replied, and touch'd my trembling ears ;
' *Fame* is no plant that grows on mortal soil,
Nor in the glistering foil
Set off to the world, nor in broad rumour lies,   80
But lives and spreads aloft by those pure eyes
And perfect witness of all-judging *Jove* ;
As he pronounces lastly on each deed,
Of so much fame in Heaven expect thy meed.'

   O Fountain *Arethuse*, and thou honour'd flood,
Smooth-sliding *Mincius*, crown'd with vocal reeds,
That strain I heard was of a higher mood :
But now my Oat proceeds,
And listens to the Herald of the Sea
That came in *Neptune's* plea ;   90
He ask'd the Waves, and ask'd the felon winds,
What hard mishap hath doom'd this gentle swain ?
And question'd every gust of ruggèd wings
That blows from off each beakèd Promontory :
They knew not of his story ;
And sage *Hippotades* their answer brings,
That not a blast was from his dungeon stray'd ;
The Air was calm, and on the level brine
Sleek *Panopë* with all her sisters play'd.
It was that fatal and perfidious Bark   100
Built in th' eclipse, and rigg'd with curses dark,
That sunk so low that sacred head of thine.

   Next *Camus*, reverend Sire, went footing slow,
His Mantle hairy, and his Bonnet sedge
Inwrought with figures dim, and on the edge
Like to that sanguine flower inscribed with woe :
Ah ! Who hath reft (quoth he) my dearest pledge ?
Last came, and last did go
The Pilot of the *Galilean* lake ;

sanguine flower] Hyacinth*.   pledge]=child.

Two massy Keys he bore of metals twain,   110
(The Golden opes, the Iron shuts amain);
He shook his Mitred locks, and stern bespake :
How well could I have spared for thee, young swain,
Enow of such as for their bellies' sake
Creep, and intrude, and climb into the fold !
Of other care they little reckoning make
Than how to scramble at the shearers' feast,
And shove away the worthy bidden guest ;
Blind mouths ! that scarce themselves know how to hold
A Sheep-hook, or have learn'd ought else the least   120
That to the faithful Herdman's art belongs !
What recks it them ?   What need they ?   They are
        sped ;
And when they list, their lean and flashy songs
Grate on their scrannel Pipes of wretched straw ;
The hungry Sheep look up, and are not fed,
But swoln with wind and the rank mist they draw
Rot inwardly, and foul contagion spread :
Besides what the grim Wolf with privy paw
Daily devours apace, and nothing said ;
But that two-handed engine at the door   130
Stands ready to smite once, and smite no more.
    Return, *Alpheus*, the dread voice is past
That shrunk thy streams ; Return, *Sicilian* Muse,
And call the Vales, and bid them hither cast
Their Bells and Flowerets of a thousand hues.
Ye valleys low, where the mild whispers use
Of shades, and wanton winds, and gushing brooks,
On whose fresh lap the swart Star sparely looks,
Throw hither all your quaint enamel'd eyes,
That on the green turf suck the honey'd showers,   140
And purple all the ground with vernal flowers.
Bring the rathe Primrose that forsaken dies,

sped] provided for.   scrannel] meagre and shrill.
Wolf] Roman church.   use] dwell.   rathe] early.

The tufted Crow-toe, and pale Jessamine,
The white Pink, and the Pansy freakt with jet,
The glowing Violet,
The Musk-rose, and the well-attired Woodbine,
With Cowslips wan that hang the pensive head,
And every flower that sad embroidery wears :
Bid *Amaranthus* all his beauty shed,
And Daffadillies fill their cups with tears   150
To strew the Laureat Hearse where *Lycid* lies.
For, so to interpose a little ease,
Let our frail thoughts dally with false surmise.
Ay me ! Whilst thee the shores, and sounding Seas
Wash far away, where'er thy bones are hurl'd,
Whether beyond the stormy *Hebrides*,
Where thou perhaps under the whelming tide
Visit'st the bottom of the monstrous world ;
Or whether thou, to our moist vows deny'd,
Sleep'st by the fable of *Bellerus* old,   160
Where the great Vision of the guarded Mount
Looks toward *Namancos* and *Bayona's* hold ;—
Look homeward, Angel, now, and melt with ruth :
And, O ye *Dolphins*, waft the hapless youth !

Weep no more, woeful Shepherds, weep no more,
For *Lycidas*, your sorrow, is not dead,
Sunk though he be beneath the watery floor ;
So sinks the day-star in the Ocean-bed,
And yet anon repairs his drooping head,
And tricks his beams, and with new spangled Ore   170
Flames in the forehead of the morning sky :
So *Lycidas* sunk low, but mounted high
Through the dear might of Him that walk'd the waves ;
Where, other groves and other streams along,
With *Nectar* pure his oozy Locks he laves,
And hears the unexpressive nuptial Song,

In the blest Kingdoms meek of joy and love.
There entertain him all the Saints above,
In solemn troops, and sweet Societies
That sing, and singing in their glory move,   180
And wipe the tears for ever from his eyes.
Now, *Lycidas*, the Shepherds weep no more ;
Henceforth thou art the Genius of the shore
In thy large recompense, and shalt be good
To all that wander in that perilous flood.

  Thus sang the uncouth Swain to th' Oaks and rills,
While the still morn went out with Sandals gray ;
He touch'd the tender stops of various Quills,
With eager thought warbling his *Dorick* lay :
And now the Sun had stretch'd out all the hills,   190
And now was dropt into the Western bay ;
At last he rose, and twitch'd his Mantle blue :
To-morrow to fresh Woods, and Pastures new.

Milton.

131

When I would muse in boyhood
  The wild green woods among,
And nurse resolves and fancies
  Because the world was young,
It was not foes to conquer,
  Nor sweethearts to be kind,
But it was friends to die for
  That I would seek and find.

I sought them far and found them,
  The sure, the straight, the brave,
The hearts I lost my own to,
  The souls I could not save.

quills] reeds.   doric] pastoral.

They braced their belts about them,
  They cross'd in ships the sea,
They sought and found six feet of ground,
  And there they died for me.
A. E. Housman.

132   *Eve to Adam*

. . . With thee conversing I forget all time,
All seasons and their change, all please alike.
Sweet is the breath of morn, her rising sweet,
With charm of earliest Birds ; pleasant the Sun
When first on this delightful Land he spreads
His orient Beams, on herb, tree, fruit, and flower,
Glistering with dew ; fragrant the fertile earth
After soft showers ; and sweet the coming on
Of grateful Evening mild ; then silent Night
With this her solemn Bird and this fair Moon,
And these the Gems of Heav'n, her starry train.
But neither breath of Morn when she ascends
With charm of earliest Birds, nor rising Sun
On this delightful land, nor herb, fruit, flower,
Glistering with dew, nor fragrance after showers,
Nor grateful Evening mild, nor silent Night
With this her solemn Bird, nor walk by Moon,
Or glittering Star-light without thee is sweet. . . .
Milton.

133

WHEN to the sessions of sweet silent thought
I summon up remembrance of things past,
I sigh the lack of many a thing I sought,
And with old woes new wail my dear time's waste :

sessions] judicial sittings, holding a privy session with myself.

K

Then can I drown an eye, unused to flow,
For precious friends hid in death's dateless night,
And weep afresh love's long since cancell'd woe,
And moan the expense of many a vanish'd sight :
Then can I grieve at grievances foregone,
And heavily from woe to woe tell o'er
The sad account of fore-bemoanèd moan,
Which I new pay as if not paid before.
    But if the while I think on thee, dear friend,
    All losses are restored and sorrows end.
                                Shakespeare.

134

WHEN, in disgrace with fortune and men's eyes,
I all alone beweep my outcast state
And trouble deaf heaven with my bootless cries
And look upon myself and curse my fate,
Wishing me like to one more rich in hope,
Featured like him, like him with friends possess'd,
Desiring this man's art, and that man's scope,
With what I most enjoy contented least ;
Yet in these thoughts myself almost despising,
Haply I think on thee,—and then my state,
Like to the lark at break of day arising
From sullen earth, sings hymns at heaven's gate ;
    For thy sweet love remember'd such wealth brings,
    That then I scorn to change my state with kings.
                                Shakespeare.

135 *From 'Christabel'* *

.   .   .   .   .   .

    Alas ! they had been friends in youth ;
    But whispering tongues can poison truth ;
    And constancy lives in realms above ;
    And life is thorny ; and youth is vain ;

foregone] that have gone by.   bootless] profitless.

And to be wroth with one we love
Doth work like madness in the brain.
And thus it chanced, as I divine,
With Roland and Sir Leoline.
Each spake words of high disdain
And insult to his heart's best brother :
They parted—ne'er to meet again !
But never either found another
To free the hollow heart from paining—
They stood aloof, the scars remaining,
Like cliffs that had been rent asunder ;
A dreary sea now flows between ;—
But neither heat, nor frost, nor thunder,
Shall wholly do away, I ween,
The marks of that which once hath been. . . .

Coleridge.

136   *Brutus and Cassius*
From *Julius Cæsar*, Act IV.

SCENE III.   Brutus' Tent

Enter Brutus *and* Cassius.

Cas. That you have wrong'd me doth appear in this :
You have condemn'd and noted Lucius Pella
For taking bribes here of the Sardians ;
Wherein my letters, praying on his side,
Because I knew the man, were slighted off.
    Bru. You wrong'd yourself to write in such a case.
    Cas. In such a time as this it is not meet
That every nice offence should bear his comment.
    Bru. Let me tell you, Cassius, you yourself
Are much condemn'd to have an itching palm ;
To sell and mart your offices for gold
To undeservers.

mart] market, make merchandise of.

CAS.   I an itching palm !
You know that you are Brutus that speaks this,
Or, by the gods, this speech were else your last.

    BRU. The name of Cassius honours this corruption,
And chastisement doth therefore hide his head.

    CAS. Chastisement !

    BRU. Remember March, the ides of March re-
      member :
Did not great Julius bleed for justice' sake ?
What villain touch'd his body, that did stab,
And not for justice ?   What, shall one of us,
That struck the foremost man of all this world
But for supporting robbers, shall we now
Contaminate our fingers with base bribes,
And sell the mighty space of our large honours
For so much trash as may be graspèd thus ?
I had rather be a dog, and bay the moon,
Than such a Roman.

    CAS.   Brutus, bay not me ;
I 'll not endure it : you forget yourself,
To hedge me in ; I am a soldier, I,
Older in practice, abler than yourself
To make conditions.

    BRU.   Go to ; you are not, Cassius.

    CAS. I am.

    BRU. I say you are not.

    CAS. Urge me no more, I shall forget myself ;
Have mind upon your health, tempt me no farther.

    BRU. Away, slight man !

    CAS. Is 't possible ?

    BRU.   Hear me, for I will speak.
Must I give way and room to your rash choler ?
Shall I be frighted when a madman stares ?

    CAS. O ye gods, ye gods ! must I endure all this ?

    BRU. All this ? ay, more : fret till your proud heart
      break ;

Go show your slaves how choleric you are,
And make your bondmen tremble.   Must I budge ?
Must I observe you ? must I stand and crouch
Under your testy humour ?   By the gods,
You shall digest the venom of your spleen,
Though it do split you ; for, from this day forth,
I 'll use you for my mirth, yea, for my laughter,
When you are waspish.

    Cas.   Is it come to this ?

    Bru. You say you are a better soldier :
Let it appear so ; make your vaunting true,
And it shall please me well : for mine own part,
I shall be glad to learn of noble men.

    Cas. You wrong me every way ; you wrong me,
       Brutus ;
I said, an elder soldier, not a better :
Did I say, better ?

    Bru.   If you did, I care not.

    Cas. When Cæsar lived, he durst not thus have moved
       me.

    Bru. Peace, peace ! you durst not so have tempted
       him.

    Cas. I durst not !

    Bru. No.

    Cas. What ! durst not tempt him !

    Bru.   For your life you durst not.

    Cas. Do not presume too much upon my love ;
I may do that I shall be sorry for.

    Bru. You have done that you should be sorry for.
There is no terror, Cassius, in your threats ;
For I am arm'd so strong in honesty
That they pass by me as the idle wind,
Which I respect not.   I did send to you
For certain sums of gold, which you denied me :
For I can raise no money by vile means :

respect not] regard not.

By heaven, I had rather coin my heart,
And drop my blood for drachmas, than to wring
From the hard hands of peasants their vile trash
By any indirection : I did send
To you for gold to pay my legions,
Which you denied me : was that done like Cassius ?
Should I have answer'd Caius Cassius so ?
When Marcus Brutus grows so covetous,
To lock such rascal counters from his friends,
Be ready, gods, with all your thunderbolts,
Dash him to pieces !

    Cas.   I denied you not.

    Bru. You did.

    Cas.   I did not : he was but a fool
That brought my answer back.   Brutus hath rived my
    heart :
A friend should bear his friend's infirmities,
But Brutus makes mine greater than they are.

    Bru. I do not, till you practise them on me.

    Cas. You love me not.

    Bru.   I do not like your faults.

    Cas. A friendly eye could never see such faults.

    Bru. A flatterer's would not, though they do appear
As huge as high Olympus.

    Cas. Come, Antony, and young Octavius, come,
Revenge yourselves alone on Cassius,
For Cassius is aweary of the world ;
Hated by one he loves ; braved by his brother ;
Check'd like a bondman ; all his faults observed,
Set in a note-book, learn'd, and conn'd by rote,
To cast into my teeth. O, I could weep
My spirit from mine eyes ! There is my dagger,
And here my naked breast ; within, a heart
Dearer than Plutus' mine, richer than gold :
If that thou be'st a Roman, take it forth ;

    indirection] crooked courses.   to lock] as to lock.

I, that denied thee gold, will give my heart :
Strike, as thou didst at Cæsar ; for I know,
When thou didst hate him worst, thou lovedst him
  better
Than ever thou lovedst Cassius.

BRU.   Sheathe your dagger :
Be angry when you will, it shall have scope ;
Do what you will, dishonour shall be humour.
O Cassius, you are yokèd with a lamb
That carries anger as the flint bears fire,
Who, much enforcèd, shows a hasty spark
And straight is cold again.

CAS.   Hath Cassius lived
To be but mirth and laughter to his Brutus,
When grief and blood ill-temper'd vexeth him ?

BRU. When I spoke that, I was ill-temper'd too.

CAS. Do you confess so much ?   Give me your hand.

BRU. And my heart too.

CAS.   O Brutus !

BRU.   What 's the matter ?

CAS. Have not you love enough to bear with me,
When that rash humour which my mother gave me
Makes me forgetful ?

BRU.   Yes, Cassius ; and from henceforth,
When you are over-earnest with your Brutus,
He 'll think your mother chides, and leave you so.

                                        Shakespeare.

137   *The Dying Gladiator*

  .   .   .   .   .

  I see before me the Gladiator lie ;
  He leans upon his hand—his manly brow
  Consents to death, but conquers agony,
    And his droop'd head sinks gradually low—

humour] the natural temper that a man is born with.

And through his side the last drops, ebbing slow
From the red gash, fall heavy, one by one,
Like the first of a thunder-shower ; and now
The arena swims around him—he is gone,
Ere ceased the inhuman shout which hail'd the wretch
    who won.

He heard it, but he heeded not—his eyes
Were with his heart, and that was far away ;
He reck'd not of the life he lost, nor prize,
But where his rude hut by the Danube lay,
There were his young barbarians all at play,
There was their Dacian mother—he, their sire,
Butcher'd to make a Roman holiday !—
All this rush'd with his blood—Shall he expire
And unavenged ?—Arise ! ye Goths, and glut your
    ire ! . . .

                           *Byron.**

138

On Wenlock Edge the wood 's in trouble ;
    His forest fleece the Wrekin heaves ;
The gale, it plies the saplings double,
    And thick on Severn snow the leaves.

'Twould blow like this through holt and hanger
    When Uricon the city stood :
'Tis the old wind in the old anger,
    But then it thresh'd another wood.

Then, 'twas before my time, the Roman
    At yonder heaving hill would stare :
The blood that warms an English yeoman,
    The thoughts that hurt him, they were there.

There, like the wind through woods in riot,
  Through him the gale of life blew high ;
The tree of man was never quiet :
  Then 'twas the Roman, now 'tis I.

The gale, it plies the saplings double,
  It blows so hard, 'twill soon be gone :
To-day the Roman and his trouble
  Are ashes under Uricon.

A. E. Housman.

139   *A Prophecy*

From *Locksley Hall*

.   .   .   .

For I dipt into the future, far as human eye could see,
Saw the Vision of the world, and all the wonder that
    would be ;

Saw the heavens fill with commerce, argosies of magic
    sails,
Pilots of the purple twilight, dropping down with costly
    bales ;

Heard the heavens fill with shouting, and there rain'd
    a ghastly dew
From the nations' airy navies grappling in the central
    blue ;

Far along the world-wide whisper of the south-wind
    rushing warm,
With the standards of the peoples plunging thro' the
    thunderstorm ;

Till the war-drum throbb'd no longer, and the battle-
    flags were furl'd
In the Parliament of man, the Federation of the
    world. . . .

Tennyson, 1842.

140* *On first looking into Chapman's Homer*

Much have I travell'd in the realms of gold,
  And many goodly states and kingdoms seen ;
  Round many western islands have I been
Which bards in fealty to Apollo hold.
Oft of one wide expanse had I been told
  That deep-brow'd Homer ruled as his demesne ;
  Yet did I never breathe its pure serene
Till I heard Chapman speak out loud and bold :
Then felt I like some watcher of the skies
  When a new planet swims into his ken ;
Or like stout Cortez when with eagle eyes
  He stared at the Pacific—and all his men
Look'd at each other with a wild surmise—
  Silent, upon a peak in Darien.

Keats.

141 *Cargoes*

Quinquereme of Nineveh from distant Ophir
Rowing home to haven in sunny Palestine,
      With a cargo of ivory
      And apes and peacocks,
Sandalwood, cedarwood, and sweet white wine.

Stately Spanish galleon coming from the Isthmus,
Dipping through the Tropics by the palm-green shores
      With a cargo of diamonds,
      Emeralds, amethysts,
Topazes, and cinnamon, and gold moidores.

Quinquereme] a ship with five banks of oars.

Dirty British coaster with a salt-caked smoke-stack
Butting through the Channel in the mad March days
      With a cargo of Tyne coal,
         Road rails, pig-lead,
Firewood, ironware, and cheap tin trays.

John Masefield.

142   *The Old Ships*

I HAVE seen old ships sail like swans asleep
Beyond the village which men still call Tyre,
With leaden age o'ercargo'd, dipping deep
For Famagusta and the hidden sun
That rings black Cyprus with a lake of fire ;
And all those ships were certainly so old
Who knows how oft with squat and noisy gun,
Questing brown slaves or Syrian oranges,
The pirate Genoese
Hell-raked them till they roll'd
Blood, water, fruit and corpses up the hold.
But now through friendly seas they softly run,
Painted the mid-sea blue or shore-sea green,
Still pattern'd with the vine and grapes in gold.

But I have seen
Pointing her shapely shadows from the dawn
And image tumbled on a rose-swept bay
A drowsy ship of some yet older day ;
And, wonder's breath indrawn,
Thought I—who knows—who knows—but in that same
(Fish'd up beyond Ææa, patch'd up new
—Stern painted brighter blue—)
That talkative, bald-headed seaman came
(Twelve patient comrades sweating at the oar)
From Troy's doom-crimson shore,

      that talkative seaman] Ulysses.

And with great lies about his wooden horse
Set the crew laughing and forgot his course.

It was so old a ship—who knows, who knows ?
—And yet so beautiful, I watch'd in vain
To see the mast burst open with a rose,
And the whole deck put on its leaves again.

Flecker.

143*

THE world is too much with us ; late and soon,
Getting and spending, we lay waste our powers :
Little we see in Nature that is ours ;
We have given our hearts away, a sordid boon !
This Sea that bares her bosom to the moon ;
The winds that will be howling at all hours,
And are up-gather'd now like sleeping flowers ;
For this, for everything, we are out of tune ;
It moves us not.—Great God ! I 'd rather be
A Pagan suckled in a creed outworn ;
So might I, standing on this pleasant lea,
Have glimpses that would make me less forlorn ;
Have sight of Proteus rising from the sea ;
Or hear old Triton blow his wreathèd horn.

Wordsworth.

144   *Song*

I

RARELY, rarely, comest thou,
    Spirit of Delight !
Wherefore hast thou left me now
    Many a day and night ?
Many a weary night and day
'Tis since thou art fled away.

II

How shall ever one like me
   Win thee back again ?
With the joyous and the free
   Thou wilt scoff at pain.
Spirit false ! thou hast forgot
   All but those who need thee not.

III

As a lizard with the shade
   Of a trembling leaf,
Thou with sorrow art dismay'd ;
   Even the sighs of grief
Reproach thee, that thou art not near,
And reproach thou wilt not hear.

IV

Let me set my mournful ditty
   To a merry measure ;
Thou wilt never come for pity,
   Thou wilt come for pleasure ;
Pity then will cut away
Those cruel wings, and thou wilt stay.

V

I love all that thou lovest,
   Spirit of Delight !
The fresh Earth in new leaves dress'd,
   And the starry night ;
Autumn evening, and the morn
When the golden mists are born.

VI

I love snow, and all the forms
   Of the radiant frost ;

I love waves, and winds, and storms,
 Everything almost
Which is Nature's, and may be
Untainted by man's misery.

VII

I love tranquil solitude,
 And such society
As is quiet, wise, and good ;
 Between thee and me
What difference ? but thou dost possess
The things I seek, not love them less.

VIII

I love Love—though he has wings,
 And like light can flee,
But above all other things,
 Spirit, I love thee—
Thou art love and life ! Oh, come,
Make once more my heart thy home.

       Shelley.

145*   *Music*

I

I PANT for the music which is divine,
 My heart in its thirst is a dying flower ;
Pour forth the sound like enchanted wine,
 Loosen the notes in a silver shower ;
Like a herbless plain, for the gentle rain,
I gasp, I faint, till they wake again.

II

Let me drink of the spirit of that sweet sound,
 More, oh more,—I am thirsting yet ;
It loosens the serpent which care has bound
 Upon my heart to stifle it ;

The dissolving strain, through every vein,
  Passes into my heart and brain. . . .

                  Shelley.

146   *Ode to the West Wind*

I

O WILD West Wind, thou breath of Autumn's being,
Thou, from whose unseen presence the leaves dead
Are driven, like ghosts from an enchanter fleeing,

Yellow, and black, and pale, and hectic red,
Pestilence-stricken multitudes : O thou,
Who chariotest to their dark wintry bed

The wingèd seeds, where they lie cold and low,
Each like a corpse within its grave, until
Thine azure sister of the Spring shall blow

Her clarion o'er the dreaming earth, and fill
(Driving sweet buds like flocks to feed in air)
With living hues and odours plain and hill :

Wild Spirit, which art moving everywhere ;
Destroyer and preserver ; hear, O hear !

II

Thou on whose stream, mid the steep sky's commotion,
Loose clouds like earth's decaying leaves are shed,
Shook from the tangled boughs of Heaven and Ocean,

Angels of rain and lightning : there are spread
On the blue surface of thine aëry surge,
Like the bright hair uplifted from the head

        shook] shaken.

Of some fierce Mænad, even from the dim verge
Of the horizon to the zenith's height,
The locks of the approaching storm.   Thou dirge

Of the dying year, to which this closing night
Will be the dome of a vast sepulchre,
Vaulted with all thy congregated might

Of vapours, from whose solid atmosphere
Black rain, and fire, and hail will burst : O hear !

III

Thou who didst waken from his summer dreams
The blue Mediterranean, where he lay,
Lull'd by the coil of his crystálline streams,

Beside a pumice isle in Baiæ's bay,
And saw in sleep old palaces and towers
Quivering within the wave's intenser day,

All overgrown with azure moss and flowers
So sweet, the sense faints picturing them !   Thou
For whose path the Atlantic's level powers

Cleave themselves into chasms, while far below
The sea-blooms and the oozy woods which wear
The sapless foliage of the ocean, know

Thy voice, and suddenly grow gray with fear,
And tremble and despoil themselves : O hear !

IV

If I were a dead leaf thou mightest bear ;
If I were a swift cloud to fly with thee ;
A wave to pant beneath thy power, and share

Mænad] mad priestess of Bacchus.

The impulse of thy strength, only less free
Than thou, O uncontrollable ! If even
I were as in my boyhood, and could be

The comrade of thy wanderings over Heaven,
As then, when to outstrip thy skiey speed
Scarce seemed a vision ; I would ne'er have striven

As thus with thee in prayer in my sore need.
O lift me as a wave, a leaf, a cloud !
I fall upon the thorns of life ! I bleed !

A heavy weight of hours has chain'd and bow'd
One too like thee : tameless, and swift, and proud.

v

Make me thy lyre, even as the forest is :
What if my leaves are falling like its own !
The tumult of thy mighty harmonies

Will take from both a deep, autumnal tone,
Sweet though in sadness. Be thou, Spirit fierce,
My spirit ! Be thou me, impetuous one !

Drive my dead thoughts over the universe
Like wither'd leaves to quicken a new birth !
And, by the incantation of this verse,

Scatter, as from an unextinguish'd hearth
Ashes and sparks, my words among mankind !
Be through my lips to unawaken'd earth

The trumpet of a prophecy ! O Wind,
If Winter comes, can Spring be far behind ?

Shelley.

L

147   *Ode on a Grecian Urn*

I

THOU still unravish'd bride of quietness,
    Thou foster-child of silence and slow time,
Sylvan historian, who canst thus express
    A flowery tale more sweetly than our rhyme :
What leaf-fringed legend haunts about thy shape
    Of deities or mortals, or of both,
        In Tempe or the dales of Arcady ?
    What men or gods are these ?   What maidens loth ?
What mad pursuit ?   What struggle to escape ?
        What pipes and timbrels ?   What wild ecstasy ?

II

Heard melodies are sweet, but those unheard
    Are sweeter ; therefore, ye soft pipes, play on ;
Not to the sensual ear, but, more endear'd,
    Pipe to the spirit ditties of no tone :
Fair youth, beneath the trees, thou canst not leave
    Thy song, nor ever can those trees be bare ;
        Bold Lover, never, never canst thou kiss,
    Though winning near the goal—yet, do not grieve ;
        She cannot fade, though thou hast not thy bliss,
    For ever wilt thou love, and she be fair !

III

Ah, happy, happy boughs ! that cannot shed
    Your leaves, nor ever bid the Spring adieu ;
And, happy melodist, unwearièd,
    For ever piping songs for ever new ;
More happy love ! more happy, happy love !
    For ever warm and still to be enjoy'd,

Tempe]*,

For ever panting, and for ever young ;
All breathing human passion far above,
   That leaves a heart high-sorrowful and cloy'd,
     A burning forehead, and a parching tongue.

IV

Who are these coming to the sacrifice ?
   To what green altar, O mysterious priest,
Lead'st thou that heifer lowing at the skies,
   And all her silken flanks with garlands drest ?
What little town by river or sea shore,
   Or mountain-built with peaceful citadel,
     Is emptied of its folk, this pious morn ?
And, little town, thy streets for evermore
   Will silent be ; and not a soul to tell
     Why thou art desolate, can e'er return.

V

O Attic shape !   Fair attitude ! with brede
   Of marble men and maidens overwrought,
With forest branches and the trodden weed ;
   Thou, silent form, dost tease us out of thought
As doth eternity : Cold Pastoral !
   When old age shall this generation waste,
     Thou shalt remain, in midst of other woe
   Than ours, a friend to man, to whom thou say'st,
' Beauty is truth, truth beauty,'—that is all
     Ye know on earth, and all ye need to know.
                    Keats.

brede] braid, embroidery, band of ornament.

148 *Farewell* *

.   .   .   .   .

Look thy last on all things lovely,
Every hour.   Let no night
Seal thy sense in deathly slumber
   Till to delight
Thou have paid thy utmost blessing ;
Since that all things thou would'st praise
Beauty took from those who loved them
   In other days.

Walter de la Mare.

149

BREAK, break, break,
   On thy cold gray stones, O Sea !
And I would that my tongue could utter
   The thoughts that arise in me.

O well for the fisherman's boy,
   That he shouts with his sister at play !
O well for the sailor lad,
   That he sings in his boat on the bay !

And the stately ships go on
   To their haven under the hill ;
But O for the touch of a vanish'd hand,
   And the sound of a voice that is still !

Break, break, break,
   At the foot of thy crags, O Sea !
But the tender grace of a day that is dead
   Will never come back to me.

Tennyson.

150 *The Light of Other Days*

OFT in the stilly night
　Ere slumber's chain has bound me,
Fond Memory brings the light
　Of other days around me :
　　The smiles, the tears
　　Of boyhood's years,
　The words of love then spoken ;
　　The eyes that shone,
　　Now dimm'd and gone,
　The cheerful hearts now broken !
Thus in the stilly night
　Ere slumber's chain has bound me,
Sad Memory brings the light
　Of other days around me.

When I remember all
　The friends so link'd together
I 've seen around me fall
　Like leaves in wintry weather,
　　I feel like one
　　Who treads alone
　Some banquet-hall deserted,
　　Whose lights are fled,
　　Whose garlands dead,
　And all but he departed !
Thus in the stilly night
　Ere slumber's chain has bound me,
Sad Memory brings the light
　Of other days around me.

Moore.

151* *Elegy in a Country Churchyard*

THE curfew tolls the knell of parting day,
  The lowing herd wind slowly o'er the lea,
The plowman homeward plods his weary way,
  And leaves the world to darkness and to me.

Now fades the glimmering landscape on the sight,
  And all the air a solemn stillness holds,
Save where the beetle wheels his droning flight,
  And drowsy tinklings lull the distant folds :

Save that from yonder ivy-mantled tower
  The moping owl does to the moon complain
Of such as wand'ring near her secret bower
  Molest her ancient solitary reign.

Beneath those rugged elms, that yew-tree's shade,
  Where heaves the turf in many a mould'ring heap,
Each in his narrow cell for ever laid,
  The rude Forefathers of the hamlet sleep.

The breezy call of incense-breathing Morn,
  The swallow twitt'ring from the straw-built shed,
The cock's shrill clarion, or the echoing horn,
  No more shall rouse them from their lowly bed.

For them no more the blazing hearth shall burn,
  Or busy housewife ply her evening care :
No children run to lisp their sire's return,
  Or climb his knees the envied kiss to share.

Oft did the harvest to their sickle yield,
  Their furrow oft the stubborn glebe has broke ;
How jocund did they drive their team afield !
  How bow'd the woods beneath their sturdy stroke !

Let not Ambition mock their useful toil,
   Their homely joys, and destiny obscure ;
Nor Grandeur hear with a disdainful smile
   The short and simple annals of the poor.

The boast of heraldry, the pomp of power,
   And all that beauty, all that wealth e'er gave,
Await alike th' inevitable hour :
   The paths of glory lead but to the grave.

Nor you, ye Proud, impute to These the fault,
   If Memory o'er their tomb no trophies raise,
Where through the long-drawn aisle and fretted vault
   The pealing anthem swells the note of praise.

Can storied urn or animated bust
   Back to its mansion call the fleeting breath ?
Can Honour's voice provoke the silent dust,
   Or Flattery soothe the dull cold ear of Death ?

Perhaps in this neglected spot is laid
   Some heart once pregnant with celestial fire ;
Hands that the rod of empire might have sway'd,
   Or waked to ecstasy the living lyre :

But Knowledge to their eyes her ample page
   Rich with the spoils of time did ne'er unroll ;
Chill Penury repress'd their noble rage,
   And froze the genial current of the soul.

Full many a gem of purest ray serene
   The dark unfathom'd caves of ocean bear :
Full many a flower is born to blush unseen,
   And waste its sweetness on the desert air.

fretted] carven.
storied urn] sepulchral urn inscribed with epitaph.
animated] life-like.   provoke] recall to life.

Some village-Hampden, that with dauntless breast
   The little tyrant of his fields withstood,
Some mute inglorious Milton here may rest,
   Some Cromwell, guiltless of his country's blood.

Th' applause of list'ning senates to command,
   The threats of pain and ruin to despise,
To scatter plenty o'er a smiling land,
   And read their history in a nation's eyes,

Their lot forbad : nor circumscribed alone
   Their growing virtues, but their crimes confined ;
Forbad to wade through slaughter to a throne,
   And shut the gates of mercy on mankind ;

[The struggling pangs of conscious truth to hide,
   To quench the blushes of ingenuous shame,
Or heap the shrine of Luxury and Pride
   With incense kindled at the Muse's flame.]

Far from the madding crowd's ignoble strife,
   Their sober wishes never learn'd to stray ;
Along the cool sequester'd vale of life
   They kept the noiseless tenour of their way.

[Yet ev'n these bones from insult to protect
   Some frail memorial still erected nigh,
With uncouth rhymes and shapeless sculpture deck'd,
   Implores the passing tribute of a sigh.]

Their name, their years, spelt by th' unletter'd Muse,
   The place of fame and elegy supply :
And many a holy text around she strews
   That teach the rustic moralist to die.

[For who, to dumb Forgetfulness a prey,
   This pleasing anxious being e'er resign'd,
Left the warm precincts of the cheerful day,
   Nor cast one longing lingering look behind ?

On some fond breast the parting soul relies,
   Some pious drops the closing eye requires ;
Ev'n from the tomb the voice of Nature cries,
   Ev'n in our ashes live their wonted fires.]

For thee, who, mindful of th' unhonour'd Dead,
   Dost in these lines their artless tale relate ;
If chance, by lonely contemplation led,
   Some kindred spirit shall inquire thy fate,—

Haply some hoary-headed swain may say,
   ' Oft have we seen him at the peep of dawn
Brushing with hasty steps the dews away
   To meet the sun upon the upland lawn.

' There at the foot of yonder nodding beech
   That wreathes its old fantastic roots so high,
His listless length at noontide would he stretch,
   And pore upon the brook that babbles by.

' Hard by yon wood, now smiling as in scorn,
   Mutt'ring his wayward fancies he would rove,
Now drooping, woeful wan, like one forlorn,
   Or crazed with care, or cross'd in hopeless love.

' One morn I miss'd him on the custom'd hill,
   Along the heath, and near his favourite tree ;
Another came ; nor yet beside the rill,
   Nor up the lawn, nor at the wood was he ;

For thee, who] the poet addresses himself.   in these lines] the Elegy.

'The next, with dirges due in sad array
  Slow through the church-way path we saw him
    borne :—
Approach and read (for thou canst read) the lay
  Graved on the stone beneath yon aged thorn.'

The Epitaph

Here rests his head upon the lap of Earth
  A Youth, to Fortune and to Fame unknown ;
Fair Science frown'd not on his humble birth,
  And Melancholy mark'd him for her own.

Large was his bounty, and his soul sincere ;
  Heaven did a recompense as largely send :
He gave to Misery all he had, a tear,
  He gain'd from Heaven, 'twas all he wish'd, a friend.

No farther seek his merits to disclose,
  Or draw his frailties from their dread abode,
(There they alike in trembling hope repose,)
  The bosom of his Father and his God.

                                        Gray, 1750.

152 *Written in Northampton County Asylum*

I AM ! yet what I am who cares, or knows ?
  My friends forsake me like a memory lost.
I am the self-consumer of my woes ;
  They rise and vanish, an oblivious host,
Shadows of life, whose very soul is lost.
And yet I am—I live—though I am toss'd

Into the nothingness of scorn and noise,
   Into the living sea of waking dream,
Where there is neither sense of life, nor joys,
   But the huge shipwreck of my own esteem
And all that 's dear. Even those I loved the best
Are strange—nay, they are stranger than the rest.

I long for scenes where man has never trod—
   For scenes where woman never smiled or wept—
There to abide with my Creator, God,
   And sleep as I in childhood sweetly slept,
Full of high thoughts, unborn. So let me lie,—
   The grass below ; above, the vaulted sky.

                      Clare.

153

    Why fadest thou in death,
        Oh yellow waning tree ?
    Gentle is autumn's breath,
        And green the oak by thee.

    But with each wind that sighs
        The leaves from thee take wing ;
    And bare thy branches rise
        Above their drifted ring.

                      Dixon.

154 *Stanzas written in dejection near Naples**

               I

    The sun is warm, the sky is clear,
        The waves are dancing fast and bright,
    Blue isles and snowy mountains wear
        The purple noon's transparent might,

The breath of the moist earth is light
Around its unexpanded buds ;
  Like many a voice of one delight,
The winds, the birds, the ocean floods,
The City's voice itself, is soft like Solitude's.

II

I see the Deep's untrampled floor
  With green and purple seaweeds strown ;
I see the waves upon the shore,
  Like light dissolved in star-showers, thrown :
  I sit upon the sands alone ;—
The lightning of the noontide ocean
  Is flashing round me, and a tone
Arises from its measured motion,
How sweet ! did any heart now share in my emotion.

III

Alas ! I have nor hope nor health,
  Nor peace within nor calm around,
Nor that Content surpassing wealth
  The sage in meditation found,
  And walk'd with inward glory crown'd—
Nor fame, nor power, nor love, nor leisure.
  Others I see whom these surround—
Smiling they live, and call life pleasure ;—
To me that cup has been dealt in another measure.

IV

Yet now despair itself is mild,
  Even as the winds and waters are ;
I could lie down like a tired child,
  And weep away the life of care
  Which I have borne and yet must bear,

Till death like sleep might steal on me,
  And I might feel in the warm air
My cheek grow cold, and hear the sea
Breathe o'er my dying brain its last monotony. . . .
Shelley.

155*   *To Night*

I

Swiftly walk o'er the western wave,
  Spirit of Night!
Out of the misty eastern cave,
Where, all the long and lone daylight,
Thou wovest dreams of joy and fear,
Which make thee terrible and dear,—
  Swift be thy flight!

II

Wrap thy form in a mantle gray,
  Star-inwrought!
Blind with thine hair the eyes of Day;
Kiss her until she be wearied out,
Then wander o'er city, and sea, and land,
Touching all with thine opiate wand—
  Come, long-sought!

III

When I arose and saw the dawn,
  I sigh'd for thee;
When light rode high, and the dew was gone,
And noon lay heavy on flower and tree,
And the weary Day turn'd to his rest,
Lingering like an unloved guest,
  I sigh'd for thee.

IV

Thy brother Death came, and cried,
    Wouldst thou me ?
Thy sweet child Sleep, the filmy-eyed,
Murmur'd like a noontide bee,
Shall I nestle near thy side ?
Wouldst thou me ?—And I replied,
    No, not thee !

V

Death will come when thou art dead,
    Soon, too soon—
Sleep will come when thou art fled ;
Of neither would I ask the boon
I ask of thee, belovèd Night—
Swift be thine approaching flight,
    Come soon, soon !

                  Shelley.

156   *Ode to a Nightingale*

I

My heart aches, and a drowsy numbness pains
  My sense, as though of hemlock I had drunk,
Or emptied some dull opiate to the drains
  One minute past, and Lethe-wards had sunk :
'Tis not through envy of thy happy lot,
  But being too happy in thine happiness,—
    That thou, light-wingèd Dryad of the trees,
      In some melodious plot
Of beechen green, and shadows numberless,
  Singest of summer in full-throated ease.

II

O for a draught of vintage ! that hath been
  Cool'd a long age in the deep-delvèd earth,
Tasting of Flora and the country green,
  Dance, and Provençal song, and sunburnt mirth !
O for a beaker full of the warm South,
  Full of the true, the blushful Hippocrene,
    With beaded bubbles winking at the brim,
      And purple-stainèd mouth ;
  That I might drink, and leave the world unseen,
  And with thee fade away into the forest dim :

III

Fade far away, dissolve, and quite forget
  What thou among the leaves hast never known,
The weariness, the fever, and the fret
  Here, where men sit and hear each other groan ;
Where palsy shakes a few, sad, last gray hairs,
  Where youth grows pale, and spectre-thin, and dies ;
    Where but to think is to be full of sorrow
      And leaden-eyed despairs,
  Where Beauty cannot keep her lustrous eyes,
  Or new Love pine at them beyond to-morrow.

IV

Away ! away ! for I will fly to thee,
  Not charioted by Bacchus and his pards,
But on the viewless wings of Poesy,
  Though the dull brain perplexes and retards :
Already with thee ! tender is the night,
  And haply the Queen-Moon is on her throne,
    Cluster'd around by all her starry Fays ;
      But here there is no light,
  Save what from heaven is with the breezes blown
  Through verdurous glooms and winding mossy ways.

Hippocrene] *.

V

I cannot see what flowers are at my feet,
  Nor what soft incense hangs upon the boughs,
But, in embalmèd darkness, guess each sweet
  Wherewith the seasonable month endows
The grass, the thicket, and the fruit-tree wild ;
  White hawthorn, and the pastoral eglantine ;
    Fast-fading violets cover'd up in leaves ;
      And mid-May's eldest child,
The coming musk-rose, full of dewy wine,
  The murmurous haunt of flies on summer eves.

VI

Darkling I listen ; and for many a time
  I have been half in love with easeful Death,
Call'd him soft names in many a musèd rhyme,
  To take into the air my quiet breath :
Now more than ever seems it rich to die,
  To cease upon the midnight with no pain,
    While thou art pouring forth thy soul abroad
      In such an ecstasy !
  Still wouldst thou sing, and I have ears in vain—
    To thy high requiem become a sod.

VII

Thou wast not born for death, immortal Bird !
  No hungry generations tread thee down ;
The voice I hear this passing night was heard
  In ancient days by emperor and clown :
Perhaps the self-same song that found a path
  Through the sad heart of Ruth, when, sick for home,
    She stood in tears amid the alien corn ;
      The same that oft-times hath
Charm'd magic casements, opening on the foam
  Of perilous seas, in faery lands forlorn.

VIII

Forlorn ! the very word is like a bell
   To toll me back from thee to my sole self.
Adieu ! the fancy cannot cheat so well
   As she is famed to do, deceiving elf.
Adieu ! adieu ! thy plaintive anthem fades
   Past the near meadows, over the still stream,
      Up the hill-side ; and now 'tis buried deep
      In the next valley-glades :
Was it a vision or a waking dream ?
   Fled is that music :—Do I wake or sleep ?

Keats.

157

Into my heart an air that kills
   From yon far country blows :
What are those blue remember'd hills,
   What spires, what farms are those ?

That is the land of lost content,
   I see it shining plain,
The happy highways where I went
   And cannot come again.

A. E. Housman.

158

Music, when soft voices die,
Vibrates in the memory—
Odours, when sweet violets sicken,
Live within the sense they quicken.

Rose leaves, when the rose is dead,
Are heap'd for the belovèd's bed ;
And so thy thoughts, when thou art gone,
Love itself shall slumber on.

Shelley.

M

159* *Song of the Lotos-Eaters*

1

THERE is sweet music here that softer falls
Than petals from blown roses on the grass,
Or night-dews on still waters between walls
Of shadowy granite, in a gleaming pass ;
Music that gentlier on the spirit lies
Than tir'd eyelids upon tir'd eyes ;
Music that brings sweet sleep down from the blissful
    skies.
Here are cool mosses deep,
And thro' the moss the ivies creep,
And in the stream the long-leaved flowers weep,
And from the craggy ledge the poppy hangs in sleep.

2

Why are we weigh'd upon with heaviness,
And utterly consumed with sharp distress,
While all things else have rest from weariness ?
All things have rest : why should we toil alone,
We only toil, who are the first of things,
And make perpetual moan,
Still from one sorrow to another thrown :
Nor ever fold our wings,
And cease from wanderings,
Nor steep our brows in slumber's holy balm ;
Nor harken what the inner spirit sings,
' There is no joy but calm ! '
Why should we only toil, the roof and crown of things ?

3

Lo ! in the middle of the wood,
The folded leaf is woo'd from out the bud

With winds upon the branch, and there
Grows green and broad, and takes no care,
Sun-steep'd at noon, and in the moon
Nightly dew-fed ; and turning yellow
Falls, and floats adown the air.
Lo ! sweeten'd with the summer light,
The full-juiced apple, waxing over-mellow,
Drops in a silent autumn night.
All its allotted length of days,
The flower ripens in its place,
Ripens and fades, and falls, and hath no toil,
Fast-rooted in the fruitful soil.

4

Hateful is the dark-blue sky,
Vaulted o'er the dark-blue sea.
Death is the end of life ; ah, why
Should life all labour be ?
Let us alone.   Time driveth onward fast,
And in a little while our lips are dumb.
Let us alone.   What is it that will last ?
All things are taken from us, and become
Portions and parcels of the dreadful Past.
Let us alone.   What pleasure can we have
To war with evil ?   Is there any peace
In ever climbing up the climbing wave ?
All things have rest, and ripen toward the grave
In silence ; ripen, fall, and cease :
Give us long rest or death, dark death, or dreamful ease.

5

How sweet it were, hearing the downward stream,
With half-shut eyes ever to seem
Falling asleep in a half-dream !

To dream and dream, like yonder amber light,
Which will not leave the myrrh-bush on the height ;
To hear each other's whisper'd speech ;
Eating the Lotos day by day,
To watch the crisping ripples on the beach,
And tender curving lines of creamy spray ;
To lend our hearts and spirits wholly
To the influence of mild-minded melancholy ;
To muse and brood and live again in memory,
With those old faces of our infancy
Heap'd over with a mound of grass,
Two handfuls of white dust, shut in an urn of brass.

6

Dear is the memory of our wedded lives,
And dear the last embraces of our wives
And their warm tears : but all hath suffer'd change ;
For surely now our household hearths are cold :
Our sons inherit us : our looks are strange :
And we should come like ghosts to trouble joy.
Or else the island princes over-bold
Have eat our substance, and the minstrel sings
Before them of the ten years' war in Troy,
And our great deeds, as half-forgotten things.
Is there confusion in the little isle ?
Let what is broken so remain.
The Gods are hard to reconcile :
'Tis hard to settle order once again.
There *is* confusion worse than death,
Trouble on trouble, pain on pain,
Long labour unto aged breath,
Sore task to hearts worn out by many wars
And eyes grown dim with gazing on the pilot-stars.

Lotos] a plant in Homer's legend whose fruit produced dreaminess
and killed desire of home.

7

But, prop on beds of amaranth and moly,
How sweet (while warm airs lull us, blowing lowly)
With half-dropt eyelids still,
Beneath a heaven dark and holy,
To watch the long bright river drawing slowly
His waters from the purple hill—
To hear the dewy echoes calling
From cave to cave thro' the thick-twinèd vine—
To watch the emerald-colour'd water falling
Thro' many a wov'n acanthus-wreath divine !
Only to hear and see the far-off sparkling brine,
Only to hear were sweet, stretch'd out beneath the pine.

8

The Lotos blooms below the barren peak :
The Lotos blows by every winding creek :
All day the wind breathes low with mellower tone :
Thro' every hollow cave and alley lone
Round and round the spicy downs the yellow Lotos-dust
    is blown.
We have had enough of action, and of motion we,
Roll'd to starboard, roll'd to larboard, when the surge
    was seething free,
Where the wallowing monster spouted his foam-
    fountains in the sea.
Let us swear an oath and keep it with an equal mind,
In the hollow Lotos-land to live and lie reclined
On the hills like Gods together, careless of mankind.
For they lie beside their nectar, and the bolts are hurl'd
Far below them in the valleys, and the clouds are lightly
    curl'd
Round their golden houses, girdled with the gleaming
    world :

amaranth] a fabulous unfading flower.
moly] the herb given to Ulysses as a charm against Circe's witchcraft.

Where they smile in secret, looking over wasted lands,
Blight and famine, plague and earthquake, roaring
    deeps and fiery sands,
Clanging fights, and flaming towns, and sinking ships,
    and praying hands.
But they smile, they find a music centred in a doleful
    song
Steaming up, a lamentation and an ancient tale of
    wrong,
Like a tale of little meaning tho' the words are strong ;
Chanted from an ill-used race of men that cleave the soil,
Sow the seed, and reap the harvest with enduring toil,
Storing yearly little dues of wheat and wine and oil ;
Till they perish and they suffer—some, 'tis whisper'd—
    down in hell
Suffer endless anguish, others in Elysian valleys dwell,
Resting weary limbs at last on beds of asphodel.
Surely, surely, slumber is more sweet than toil, the shore
Than labour in the deep mid-ocean, wind and wave
    and oar ;
Oh rest ye, brother mariners, we will not wander more.
                    Tennyson, 1832.

160

    Flow down, cold rivulet, to the sea,
      Thy tribute wave deliver :
    No more by thee my steps shall be,
      For ever and for ever.

    Flow, softly flow, by lawn and lea,
      A rivulet then a river :
    Nowhere by thee my steps shall be,
      For ever and for ever.

asphodel] the flower of the Elysian fields.

But here will sigh thine alder tree,
  And here thine aspen shiver ;
And here by thee will hum the bee,
  For ever and for ever.

A thousand suns will stream on thee,
  A thousand moons will quiver ;
But not by thee my steps shall be,
  For ever and for ever.

Tennyson.

161 *The Lake Isle of Innisfree*

I WILL arise and go now, and go to Innisfree,
And a small cabin build there, of clay and wattles made ;
Nine bean-rows will I have there, a hive for the honey-
    bee,
  And live alone in the bee-loud glade.

And I shall have some peace there, for peace comes
    dropping slow,
Dropping from the veils of the morning to where the
    cricket sings ;
There midnight 's all a glimmer, and noon a purple glow,
  And evening full of the linnet's wings.

I will arise and go now, for always night and day
I hear lake-water lapping with low sounds by the shore ;
While I stand on the roadway, or on the pavements gray,
  I hear it in the deep heart's core.

W. B. Yeats.

162 *To the Rev. F. D. Maurice*

COME, when no graver cares employ,
Godfather, come and see your boy :
  Your presence will be sun in winter,
Making the little one leap for joy.

For, being of that honest few,
Who give the Fiend himself his due,
  Should eighty-thousand college-councils
Thunder ' Anathema,' friend, at you ;

Should all our churchmen foam in spite
At you, so careful of the right,
  Yet one lay-heart would give you welcome
(Take it and come) to the Isle of Wight ;

Where, far from noise and smoke of town,
I watch the twilight falling brown
  All round a careless-order'd garden
Close to the ridge of a noble down.

You 'll have no scandal while you dine,
But honest talk and wholesome wine,
  And only hear the magpie gossip
Garrulous under a roof of pine :

For groves of pine on either hand,
To break the blast of winter, stand ;
  And further on, the hoary Channel
Tumbles a billow on chalk and sand ;

Where, if below the milky steep
Some ship of battle slowly creep,
  And on thro' zones of light and shadow
Glimmer away to the lonely deep,

We might discuss the Northern sin
Which made a selfish war begin ;
  Dispute the claims, arrange the chances ;
Emperor, Ottoman, which shall win :

Or whether war's avenging rod
Shall lash all Europe into blood ;
  Till you should turn to dearer matters,
Dear to the man that is dear to God ;

How best to help the slender store,
How mend the dwellings, of the poor ;
   How gain in life, as life advances,
Valour and charity more and more.

Come, Maurice, come : the lawn as yet
Is hoar with rime, or spongy-wet ;
   But when the wreath of March has blossom'd,
Crocus, anemone, violet,

Or later, pay one visit here,
For those are few we hold as dear ;
   Nor pay but one, but come for many,
Many and many a happy year.

Tennyson, 1854.

163   *The Kingfisher*

  It was the Rainbow gave thee birth,
    And left thee all her lovely hues ;
  And, as her mother's name was Tears,
    So runs it in thy blood to choose
  For haunts the lonely pools, and keep
  In company with trees that weep.

  Go you and, with such glorious hues,
    Live with proud Peacocks in green parks ;
  On lawns as smooth as shining glass,
    Let every feather show its marks ;
  Get thee on boughs and clap thy wings
  Before the windows of proud kings.

  Nay, lovely bird, thou art not vain ;
    Thou hast no proud ambitious mind :
  I also love a quiet place
    That 's green, away from all mankind ;
  A lonely pool, and let a tree
  Sigh with her bosom over me.

W. H. Davies.

164 To Lucasta, on Going to the Wars

TELL me not, Sweet, I am unkind,
   That from the nunnery
Of thy chaste breast and quiet mind
   To war and arms I fly.

True, a new mistress now I chase,
   The first foe in the field ;
And with a stronger faith embrace
   A sword, a horse, a shield.

Yet this inconstancy is such
   As you too shall adore ;
I could not love thee, Dear, so much,
   Loved I not Honour more.

Lovelace.

165 The Volunteer

' HE leapt to arms unbidden,
   Unneeded, over-bold :
His face by earth is hidden,
   His heart in earth is cold.

' Curse on the reckless daring
   That could not wait the call,
The proud fantastic bearing
   That would be first to fall ! '

O tears of human passion,
   Blur not the image true !
This was not folly's fashion,
   This was the man we knew.

Henry Newbolt.

166

Her strong enchantments failing,
    Her towers of fear in wreck,
Her limbecks dried of poisons
    And the knife at her neck,

The Queen of air and darkness
    Begins to shrill and cry,
' O young man, O my slayer,
    To-morrow you shall die.'

O Queen of air and darkness,
    I think 'tis truth you say,
And I shall die to-morrow ;
    But you will die to-day.'

                    A. E. Housman.

167   *The Spirit's Warfare*

To find the Western path,
Right through the Gates of Wrath
        I urge my way ;
Sweet Mercy leads me on
With soft repentant moan :
        I see the break of day.

The war of swords and spears,
Melted by dewy tears,
        Exhales on high ;
The Sun is freed from fears,
And with soft grateful tears
        Ascends the sky.

                    Blake.

limbeck]=alembic, the vessel used in distilling.

168 *Song*

So, we 'll go no more a-roving
　　So late into the night,
Tho' the heart be still as loving
　　And the moon be still as bright.

For the sword outwears its sheath,
　　And the soul wears out the breast,
And the heart must pause to breathe,
　　And love itself have rest.

Tho' the night was made for loving,
　　And the day returns too soon,
Yet we 'll go no more a-roving
　　By the light of the moon.

　　　　　　　　　　Byron.

169 *Napoleon's Farewell*

Farewell to the Land where the gloom of my Glory
Arose and o'ershadow'd the earth with her name—
She abandons me now—but the page of her story,
The brightest or blackest, is fill'd with my fame.
I have warr'd with a world which vanquish'd me only
When the meteor of conquest allured me too far ;
I have coped with the nations which dread me thus
　　lonely,
The last single Captive to millions in war.

Farewell to thee, France ! when thy diadem crown'd me,
I made thee the gem and the wonder of earth,—
But thy weakness decrees I should leave as I found thee,
Decay'd in thy glory, and sunk in thy worth.
Oh ! for the veteran hearts that were wasted
In strife with the storm, when their battles were won—
Then the Eagle, whose gaze in that moment was blasted,
Had still soar'd with eyes fix'd on victory's sun !

Farewell to thee, France !—but when Liberty rallies
Once more in thy regions, remember me then—
The violet still grows in the depth of thy valleys ;
Though wither'd, thy tear will unfold it again—
Yet, yet I may baffle the hosts that surround us,
And yet may thy heart leap awake to my voice—
There are links which must break in the chain that has
    bound us,
Then turn thee and call on the Chief of thy choice.
Byron, 1816.

170   *Song from 'As You Like It'*

Blow, blow, thou winter wind,
Thou art not so unkind
    As man's ingratitude ;
Thy tooth is not so keen,
Because thou art not seen,
    Although thy breath be rude.
Heigh ho ! sing, heigh ho ! unto the green holly :
Most friendship is feigning, most loving mere folly :
    Then, heigh ho ! the holly !
    This life is most jolly.

Freeze, freeze, thou bitter sky,
That dost not bite so nigh
    As benefits forgot :
Though thou the waters warp,
Thy sting is not so sharp
    As friend remember'd not.
Heigh ho ! sing, heigh ho ! unto the green holly :
Most friendship is feigning, most loving mere folly :
    Then, heigh ho ! the holly !
    This life is most jolly.
Shakespeare.

171* *Il Penseroso*

HENCE, vain deluding joys,
    The brood of folly without father bred !
How little you bestead,
    Or fill the fixèd mind with all your toys !
Dwell in some idle brain,
    And fancies fond with gaudy shapes possess
As thick and numberless
    As the gay motes that people the Sun Beams,
Or likest hovering dreams
      The fickle Pensioners of *Morpheus'* train.   10
        But hail thou Goddess, sage and holy,
        Hail divinest Melancholy,
        Whose saintly visage is too bright
        To hit the Sense of human sight ;
        And therefore to our weaker view,
        O'erlaid with black, staid Wisdom's hue . . .
           Come, pensive Nun, devout and pure,   31
        Sober, stedfast, and demure,
        All in a robe of darkest grain,
        Flowing with majestic train,
        And sable stole of *Cypres* Lawn,
        Over thy decent shoulders drawn :
        Come, but keep thy wonted state,
        With even step, and musing gait,
        And looks commércing with the skies,
        Thy rapt soul sitting in thine eyes :   40
        There, held in holy passion still,
        Forget thyself to Marble, till
        With a sad Leaden downward cast
        Thou fix them on the earth as fast :

---

3. bestead] avail, support.   33. grain] dye.
35. Cypres Lawn] a transparent lawn or crape worn in mourning.
44. as fast] as firmly as before on heaven.

And join with thee calm Peace, and Quiet,
Spare Fast, that oft with gods doth diet,
And hears the Muses in a ring
Aye round about *Jove's* Altar sing :
And add to these retirèd Leisure,
That in trim Gardens takes his pleasure :—   50
But first, and chiefest, with thee bring
Him that yon soars on golden wing,
Guiding the fiery-wheelèd throne,
The Cherub Contemplatiòn ;
And the mute Silence hist along,
'Less *Philomel* will deign a Song
In her sweetest, saddest plight,
Smoothing the rugged brow of night,
While *Cynthia* checks her Dragon yoke,
Gently o'er the accustom'd Oak.   60
Sweet Bird, that shunn'st the noise of folly,
Most musical, most melancholy !
Thee Chauntress oft the Woods among,
I woo to hear thy even-Song ;
And missing thee, I walk unseen
On the dry smooth-shaven Green,
To behold the wandering Moon,
Riding near her highest noon,
Like one that had been led astray
Through the Heavens' wide pathless way ;   70
And oft, as if her head she bow'd,
Stooping through a fleecy cloud.
   Oft on a Plat of rising ground
I hear the far-off *Curfew* sound
Over some wide-water'd shore
Swinging slow with sullen roar ;
Or if the Air will not permit,
Some still removèd place will fit,

55. hist along! whisperingly summon with you.

Where glowing Embers through the room
Teach light to counterfeit a gloom,   80
Far from all resort of mirth,
Save the Cricket on the hearth,
Or the Bellman's drowsy charm,
To bless the doors from nightly harm.
  Or let my Lamp at midnight hour
Be seen in some high lonely Tower,
Where I may oft out-watch the *Bear*
With thrice great *Hermes*, or unsphere
The spirit of *Plato* to unfold
What Worlds, or what vast Regions hold   90
The immortal mind that hath forsook
Her mansion in this fleshly nook :
And of those *Dæmons* that are found
In fire, air, flood, or under ground,
Whose power hath a true consent
With Planet, or with Element.
Sometime let Gorgeous Tragedy
In Scepter'd Pall come sweeping by,
Presenting *Thebes*, or *Pelops'* line,
Or the tale of *Troy* divine ;   100
Or what (though rare) of later age
Ennobled hath the Buskin'd stage.
  But, O sad Virgin, that thy power
Might raise *Musæus* from his bower,
Or bid the soul of *Orpheus* sing
Such notes as, warbled to the string,
Drew Iron tears down *Pluto's* cheek,
And made Hell grant what Love did seek.
Or call up him that left half-told
The story of *Cambuscan* bold,   110

83. charm] chanting (as in 132)=song.
88. unsphere] draw down from heaven.
102. buskined] tragic, the high-soled buskin (boot) was worn in Greek tragedy.

Of *Camball*, and of *Algarsife*,
And who had *Canacè* to wife,
That own'd the virtuous Ring and Glass,
And of the wondrous Horse of Brass
On which the *Tartar* King did ride ;
And if ought else great *Bards* beside
In sage and solemn tunes have sung
Of Turneys and of Trophies hung,
Of Forests, and enchantments drear,
Where more is meant than meets the ear.   120
    Thus Night oft see me in thy pale career,
Till civil-suited Morn appear,
Not trick'd and frounced as she was wont
With the Attic Boy to hunt,
But kercheft in a comely Cloud
While rocking Winds are piping loud,
Or usher'd with a shower still,
When the gust hath blown his fill,
Ending on the rustling Leaves
With minute drops from off the Eaves.   130
And when the Sun begins to fling
His flaring beams, me, Goddess, bring
To archèd walks of twilight groves,
And shadows brown that *Sylvan* loves
Of Pine, or monumental Oak,
Where the rude Axe with heavèd stroke
Was never heard the Nymphs to daunt,
Or fright them from their hallow'd haunt.
There in close covert by some Brook,
Where no profaner eye may look,   140
Hide me from Day's garish eye,
While the Bee with honey'd thigh,
That at her flowery work doth sing,
And the Waters murmuring,

122. civil-suited] soberly clad.   123. tricked] adorned.
123. frounced] with hair curled.   124. Attic Boy] Cephalus.
130. minute] as in ' minute-guns.'   134. brown] dusky.

N

With such consort as they keep
Entice the dewy-feather'd Sleep ;
And let some strange mysterious dream
Wave at his Wings in Airy stream
Of lively portraiture display'd,
Softly on my eye-lids laid.   150
And as I wake, sweet musick breathe
Above, about, or underneath,
Sent by some spirit to mortals good,
Or th' unseen Genius of the Wood.

 But let my due feet never fail,
To walk the studious Cloister's pale,
And love the high embowèd Roof,
With antique Pillars massy proof,
And storied Windows richly dight,
Casting a dim religious light.   160
There let the pealing Organ blow
To the full-voiced Quire below
In Service high and Anthems clear,
As may with sweetness, through mine ear,
Dissolve me into extasies,
And bring all Heav'n before mine eyes.
And may at last my weary age
Find out the peaceful hermitage,
The Hairy Gown and Mossy Cell,
Where I may sit and rightly spell   170
Of every Star that Heav'n doth shew,
And every Herb that sips the dew :
Till old experience do attain
To something like Prophetic strain.

 These pleasures, *Melancholy*, give,
And I with thee will choose to live.

Milton.

148. his wings] sleep's wings.   156. pale] enclosure.
158. proof] of great (tried) strength (adj.).
159. dight] adorned. 162. full voiced] pr. voic'd not voicèd.

172 *From the Second Hyperion*

I

. . . Turning from these with awe, once more I raised
My eyes to fathom the space every way ;
The embossèd roof, the silent massy range
Of columns north and south, ending in mist
Of nothing, then to eastward, where black gates
Were shut against the sunrise evermore.—
Then to the west I look'd, and saw far off
An image, huge of feature as a cloud,
At level of whose feet an altar slept,
To be approach'd on either side by steps
And marble balustrade, and patient travail
To count with toil the innumerable degrees.
Towards the altar sober-paced I went,
Repressing haste, as too unholy there ;
And, coming nearer, saw beside the shrine
One minist'ring ; and there arose a flame.—
When in mid-way the sickening east wind
Shifts sudden to the south, the small warm rain
Melts out the frozen incense from all flowers,
And fills the air with so much pleasant health
That even the dying man forgets his shroud ;—
Even so that lofty sacrificial fire,
Sending forth Maian incense, spread around
Forgetfulness of everything but bliss,
And clouded all the altar with soft smoke. . . .

II

. . . ' High Prophetess,' said I, ' purge off,
Benign, if so it please thee, my mind's film.'—
' None can usurp this height,' return'd that shade,
' But those to whom the miseries of the world

Maian] *

Are misery, and will not let them rest.
All else who find a haven in the world,
Where they may thoughtless sleep away their days,
If by a chance into this fane they come,
Rot on the pavement where thou rottedst half.'—
' Are there not thousands in the world,' said I,
Encouraged by the sooth voice of the shade,
' Who love their fellows even to the death,
Who feel the giant agony of the world,
And more, like slaves to poor humanity,
Labour for mortal good ?   I sure should see
Other men here ; but I am here alone.'
' Those whom thou spak'st of are no visionaries,'
Rejoin'd that voice—' They are no dreamers weak,
They seek no wonder but the human face ;
No music but a happy-noted voice—
They come not here, they have no thought to come—
And thou art here, for thou art less than they—
What benefit canst thou, or all thy tribe,
To the great world ?   Thou art a dreaming thing,
A fever of thyself ; think of the Earth ;
What bliss even in hope is there for thee ?
What haven ? every creature hath its home ;
Every sole man hath days of joy and pain,
Whether his labours be sublime or low—
The pain alone, the joy alone, distinct :
Only the dreamer venoms all his days,
Bearing more woe than all his sins deserve. . . .'

Keats.

sooth] gentle.

173 *La Belle Dame sans Merci*

O WHAT can ail thee, Knight-at-arms,
   Alone and palely loitering ?
The sedge has wither'd from the lake,
   And no birds sing.

O what can ail thee, Knight-at-arms,
   So haggard and so woe-begone ?
The squirrel's granary is full,
   And the harvest 's done.

I see a lily on thy brow
   With anguish moist and fever dew ;
And on thy cheeks a fading rose
   Fast withereth too.

I met a Lady in the meads,
   Full beautiful, a faery's child ;—
Her hair was long, her foot was light,
   And her eyes were wild.

I set her on my pacing steed,
   And nothing else saw all day long ;
For sidelong would she bend and sing
   A faery's song.

I made a garland for her head,
   And bracelets too, and fragrant zone ;
She look'd at me as she did love,
   And made sweet moan.

She found me roots of relish sweet,
   And honey wild, and manna dew ;
And sure in language strange she said—
   ' I love thee true.'

She took me to her elfin grot,
   And there she wept and sigh'd full sore,
And there I shut her wild, wild eyes
   With kisses four.

And there she lullèd me asleep,
   And there I dream'd—Ah! woe betide!
The latest dream I ever dream'd
   On the cold hill-side.

I saw pale Kings, and Princes too,
   Pale warriors, death-pale were they all;
Who cry'd—' La Belle Dame sans Merci
   Hath thee in thrall!'

I saw their starved lips in the gloam
   With horrid warning gapèd wide,
And I awoke, and found me here
   On the cold hill-side.

And this is why I sojourn here
   Alone and palely loitering,
Though the sedge is wither'd from the lake,
   And no birds sing.

                                        Keats.

174   *Song*

      TELL me where is Fancy bred,
      Or in the heart or in the head?
      How begot, how nourishèd?
            Reply, reply!
      It is engender'd in the eyes,
      With gazing fed; and Fancy dies
      In the cradle where it lies.

Let us all ring Fancy's knell :
I 'll begin it,—Ding, dong, bell.
Ding, dong, bell.

Shakespeare.

175* *L'Allegro*

Hence, loathèd Melancholy,
Of *Cerberus*, and blackest midnight born,
In *Stygian* Cave forlorn
'Mongst horrid shapes and shrieks, and sights unholy !
Find out some uncouth cell,
Where brooding darkness spreads his jealous wings,
And the night-Raven sings ;
There under *Ebon* shades, and low-brow'd Rocks,
As ragged as thy Locks,
In dark *Cimmerian* desert ever dwell.   10
But come thou Goddess fair and free,
In Heav'n yclep'd *Euphrosyne*,
And by men, heart-easing Mirth,
Whom lovely *Venus* at a birth
With two sister Graces more
To ivy-crownèd *Bacchus* bore :
Or whether (as some sager sing)
The frolick Wind that breathes the Spring
Zephyr with *Aurora* playing,
As he met her once a-Maying,   20
There on Beds of Violets blue
And fresh-blown Roses wash'd in dew,
Fill'd her with thee, a daughter fair,
So bucksom, blithe, and debonair.
    Haste thee, nymph, and bring with thee
Jest and youthful Jollity,
Quips and Cranks, and wanton Wiles,
Nods, and Becks, and Wreathèd Smiles,

24. buxom] well-favoured.   debonair] gracious.

Such as hang on *Hebe's* cheek,
And love to live in dimple sleek :   30
Sport that wrinkled Care derides,
And Laughter holding both his sides.
Come, and trip it as ye go
On the light fantastic toe ;
And in thy right hand lead with thee
The Mountain Nymph, sweet Liberty ;
And if I give thee honour due,
Mirth, admit me of thy crew,
To live with her, and live with thee,
In unreprovèd pleasures free ;   40
To hear the Lark begin his flight
And singing startle the dull night
From his watch-tower in the skies,
Till the dappled dawn doth rise ;
Then to come in spite of sorrow,
And at my window bid good-morrow,
Through the Sweet-Briar, or the Vine,
Or the twisted Eglantine ;
While the Cock with lively din
Scatters the rear of darkness thin,   50
And to the stack, or the Barn-door,
Stoutly struts his Dames before ;
Oft listening how the Hounds and horn
Cheerly rouse the slumbering morn,
From the side of some hoar Hill,
Through the high wood echoing shrill.
Some time walking not unseen
By hedge-row Elms, on Hillocks green,
Right against the Eastern gate,
Where the great Sun begins his state,   60
Robed in flames and Amber light,
The clouds in thousand Liveries dight ;

48. Eglantine] sweet-briar, here for 'honeysuckle' (?).
62. dight] adorned.

While the Plowman near at hand,
Whistles o'er the furrow'd Land,
And the Milkmaid singeth blithe,
And the Mower whets his scythe,
And every Shepherd tells his tale
Under the Hawthorn in the dale.
  Straight mine eye hath caught new pleasures
Whilst the Landskip round it measures ;   70
Russet Lawns, and Fallows gray,
Where the nibbling flocks do stray,
Mountains on whose barren breast
The labouring clouds do often rest ;
Meadows trim with Daisies pied,
Shallow Brooks, and Rivers wide :
Towers and Battlements it sees
Bosom'd high in tufted Trees,
Where perhaps some beauty lies,
The Cynosure of neighbouring eyes.   80
Hard by, a cottage chimney smokes,
From betwixt two agèd Oaks,
Where *Corydon* and *Thyrsis*, met,
Are at their savoury dinner set
Of Herbs, and other Country Messes,
Which the neat-handed *Phillis* dresses ;
And then in haste her Bower she leaves,
With *Thestylis* to bind the Sheaves ;
Or, if the earlier season lead,
To the tann'd Haycock in the Mead.   90
  Sometimes with secure delight
The upland Hamlets will invite,
When the merry Bells ring round,
And the jocund rebecks sound
To many a youth and many a maid
Dancing in the chequer'd shade ;

67. tells his tale] counts his flock.
80. cynosure] pole-star, centre of attraction.
94. rebeck] three-stringed fiddle.

And young and old come forth to play
On a sunshine Holyday,
Till the livelong daylight fail ;
Then to the spicy nut-brown Ale,   100
With stories told of many a feat,
How *Faery Mab* the junkets eat ;
She was pinch'd and pull'd, she said,
And he by Friar's Lanthorn led ;
Tells how the drudging *Goblin* swet,
To earn his Cream-bowl duly set,
When in one night, ere glimpse of morn,
His shadowy Flail hath thresh'd the Corn
That ten day-labourers could not end ;
Then lies him down the Lubber Fiend, 110
And stretch'd out all the Chimney's length,
Basks at the fire his hairy strength ;
And crop-full out of doors he flings,
Ere the first Cock his Matin rings.
Thus done the Tales, to bed they creep,
By whispering Winds soon lull'd asleep.

 Tower'd Cities please us then,
And the busy hum of men,
Where throngs of Knights and Barons bold,
In weeds of Peace high triumphs hold, 120
With store of Ladies, whose bright eyes
Rain influence, and judge the prize
Of Wit, or Arms ; while both contend
To win her Grace, whom all commend.
There let *Hymen* oft appear
In Saffron robe, with Taper clear,
And pomp, and feast, and revelry,
With mask, and antique Pageantry ;

---

102. eat] ate.
104. and he by Friar's] and he, who said he had been led astray by a
will-o'-the-wisp, tells of Robin Goodfellow. *He* and *she* are chance
speakers. 105. swet] old past tense. 120. weeds] garments.

Such sights as youthful Poets dream
On Summer eves by haunted stream.　　　130
Then to the well-trod stage anon,
If *Jonson's* learnèd Sock be on,
Or sweetest *Shakespear*, Fancy's child,
Warble his native Wood-notes wild.
　　And ever against eating Cares
Lap me in soft *Lydian* Airs
Married to immortal verse,
Such as the meeting soul may pierce
In notes, with many a winding bout
Of linkèd sweetness long drawn out,　　　140
With wanton heed and giddy cunning,
The melting voice through mazes running ;
Untwisting all the chains that tie
The hidden soul of harmony ;
That *Orpheus'* self may heave his head
From golden slumber, on a bed
Of heap'd *Elysian* flowers, and hear
Such strains as would have won the ear
Of *Pluto*, to have quite set free
His half-regain'd *Eurydice*.　　　150
　　These delights if thou canst give,
Mirth, with thee I mean to live.
　　　　　　　　　　　Milton.

176*　　　*What is Life ?*

. . . Stop and consider ! life is but a day ;
A fragile dew-drop on its perilous way
From a tree's summit : a poor Indian's sleep
While his boat hastens to the monstrous steep
Of Montmorenci.　Why so sad a moan ?
Life is the rose's hope while yet unblown ;

132. sock] the low shoe of comedy, see 171, l. 102, note on buskin.
138. meeting] coming in response.

The reading of an ever-changing tale ;
The light uplifting of a maiden's veil ;
A pigeon tumbling in clear summer air ;
A laughing school-boy, without grief or care,
Riding the springy branches of an elm. . . .

Keats.

177 *The Human Seasons*

FOUR Seasons fill the measure of the year ;
  There are four seasons in the mind of man :
He has his lusty Spring, when fancy clear
  Takes in all beauty with an easy span :
He has his Summer, when luxuriously
  Spring's honey'd cud of youthful thought he
    loves
To ruminate, and by such dreaming high
  Is nearest unto Heaven : quiet coves
His soul has in its Autumn, when his wings
  He furleth close ; contented so to look
On mists in idleness—to let fair things
  Pass by unheeded as a threshold brook :
He has his Winter too of pale misfeature,
Or else he would forego his mortal nature.

Keats.

178 *The Seven Ages of Man*

    . . . All the world's a stage,
And all the men and women merely players :
They have their exits and their entrances ;
And one man in his time plays many parts,
His acts being seven ages. At first the infant,
Mewling and puking in the nurse's arms.

Then the whining school-boy, with his satchel
And shining morning face, creeping like snail
Unwillingly to school.   And then the lover ;
Sighing like furnace, with a woeful ballad
Made to his mistress' eyebrow.   Then a soldier,
Full of strange oaths and bearded like the pard,
Jealous in honour, sudden and quick in quarrel,
Seeking the bubble reputation
Even in the cannon's mouth.   And then the justice ;
In fair round belly with good capon lined,
With eyes severe and beard of formal cut,
Full of wise saws and modern instances ;
And so he plays his part.   The sixth age shifts
Into the lean and slipper'd pantaloon,
With spectacles on nose and pouch on side,
His youthful hose, well saved, a world too wide
For his shrunk shank ; and his big manly voice,
Turning again toward childish treble, pipes
And whistles in his sound.   Last scene of all,
That ends this strange eventful history,
Is second childishness and mere oblivion,
Sans teeth, sans eyes, sans taste, sans everything.

Shakespeare.

179*

. . . Whate'er the passion, knowledge, fame, or pelf,
Not one will change his neighbour with himself.
The learn'd is happy nature to explore,
The fool is happy that he knows no more ;
The rich is happy in the plenty given,
The poor contents him with the care of Heaven.
See the blind beggar dance, the cripple sing,
The sot a hero, lunatic a king ;

pard] leopard.   his sound]*.
sans] without, pronounce as English.

The starving chemist in his golden views
Supremely blest, the poet in his muse.
   See some strange comfort every state attend,
And pride bestow'd on all, a common friend :
See some fit passion every age supply,
Hope travels through, nor quits us when we die.
   Behold the child, by nature's kindly law,
Pleased with a rattle, tickled with a straw :
Some livelier plaything gives his youth delight,
A little louder, but as empty quite :
Scarfs, garters, gold, amuse his riper stage,
And beads and prayer-books are the toys of age :
Pleased with this bauble still as that before,
Till tired he sleeps, and life's poor play is o'er. . . .

                       Pope.

180   *A Lament*

I

O world ! O life ! O time !
On whose last steps I climb,
   Trembling at that where I had stood before ;
When will return the glory of your prime ?
     No more—Oh, never more !

II

Out of the day and night
A joy has taken flight ;
   Fresh spring, and summer, and winter hoar,
Move my faint heart with grief, but with delight
     No more—Oh, never more !

                       Shelley.

181 *Time*

UNFATHOMABLE Sea ! whose waves are years,
 Ocean of Time, whose waters of deep woe
Are brackish with the salt of human tears !
 Thou shoreless flood, which in thy ebb and flow
Claspest the limits of mortality,
And sick of prey, yet howling on for more,
Vomitest thy wrecks on its inhospitable shore ;
 Treacherous in calm, and terrible in storm,
  Who shall put forth on thee,
  Unfathomable Sea ?

Shelley.

182

  . . . I have learn'd
To look on Nature, not as in the hour
Of thoughtless youth, but hearing oftentimes
The still, sad music of humanity,
Nor harsh nor grating, though of ample power
To chasten and subdue. And I have felt
A presence that disturbs me with the joy
Of elevated thoughts ; a sense sublime
Of something far more deeply interfused,
Whose dwelling is the light of setting suns,
And the round ocean and the living air,
And the blue sky, and in the mind of man :
A motion and a spirit, that impels
All thinking things, all objects of all thought,
And rolls through all things. Therefore am I still
A lover of the meadows and the woods
And mountains, and of all that we behold
From this green earth ; of all the mighty world
Of eye and ear,—both what they half create,
And what perceive ; well pleased to recognize

In Nature and the language of the sense
The anchor of my purest thoughts, the nurse,
The guide, the guardian of my heart, and soul
Of all my moral being. . . .

*Wordsworth.**

183

Know then thyself, presume not God to scan,
The proper study of mankind is Man.
Placed on this isthmus of a middle state,
A being darkly wise, and rudely great ;
With too much knowledge for the sceptic side,
With too much weakness for the Stoic's pride,
He hangs between ; in doubt to act, or rest ;
In doubt to deem himself a God, or beast ;
In doubt his mind or body to prefer ;
Born but to die, and reasoning but to err ;
Alike in ignorance, his reason such,
Whether he thinks too little, or too much :
Chaos of thought and passion, all confused ;
Still by himself abused, or disabused ;
Created half to rise, and half to fall ;
Great lord of all things, yet a prey to all ;
Sole judge of truth, in endless error hurl'd ;
The glory, jest, and riddle of the world ! . . .

*Pope.**

184 *Nature*

Because out of corruption burns the rose,
And to corruption lovely cheeks descend ;
Because with her right hand she heals the woes
Her left hand wrought, loth nor to wound nor mend :

I praise indifferent Nature, affable
To all philosophies, of each unknown ;
Though in my listening ear she leans to tell
Some private word, as if for me alone.

Still, like an artist, she her meaning hides,
Silent, while thousand tongues proclaim it clear ;
Ungrudging, her large feast for all provides ;
Tender, exultant, savage, blithe, austere,
In each man's hand she sets the proper tool,
For the wise Wisdom, Folly for the fool.

Laurence Binyon.

185   *Quiet Work*

ONE lesson, Nature, let me learn of thee,
   One lesson, which in every wind is blown,
   One lesson of two duties kept at one,
   Tho' the loud world proclaim their enmity—
Of toil unsever'd from tranquillity !
   Of labour, that in lasting fruit outgrows
   Far noisier schemes, accomplish'd in repose—
   Too great for haste, too high for rivalry !
Yes, while on earth a thousand discords ring,
   Man's fitful uproar mingling with his toil,
   Still do thy sleepless ministers move on,
   Their glorious tasks in silence perfecting !
   Still working, blaming still our vain turmoil,
   Labourers that shall not fail, when man is gone.

Arnold.

186   *The House Beautiful*

   A naked house, a naked moor,
   A shivering pool before the door,
   A garden bare of flowers and fruit
   And poplars at the garden foot :
   Such is the place that I live in,
   Bleak without and bare within.

Yet shall your ragged moor receive
The incomparable pomp of eve,
And the cold glories of the dawn
Behind your shivering trees be drawn ;
And when the wind from place to place
Doth the unmoor'd cloud-galleons chase,
Your garden gloom and gleam again,
With leaping sun, with glancing rain.
Here shall the wizard moon ascend
The heavens, in the crimson end
Of day's declining splendour ; here
The army of the stars appear.
The neighbour hollows, dry or wet,
Spring shall with tender flowers beset ;
And oft the morning muser see
Larks rising from the broomy lea,
And every fairy-wheel and thread
Of cobweb dew-bediamonded.
When daisies go, shall winter time
Silver the simple grass with rime ;
Autumnal frosts enchant the pool
And make the cart-ruts beautiful ;
And when snow-bright the moor expands,
How shall your children clap their hands !
To make this earth, our hermitage,
A cheerful and a changeful page,
God's bright and intricate device
Of days and seasons doth suffice.

Stevenson.

187   *The Rainbow*

My heart leaps up when I behold
A rainbow in the sky :
So was it when my life began ;
So is it now I am a man :

So be it when I shall grow old,
   Or let me die !
The Child is father of the Man ;
And I could wish my days to be
Bound each to each by natural piety.

Wordsworth,

188   *The Leech-gatherer**

I

THERE was a roaring in the wind all night ;
The rain came heavily and fell in floods ;
But now the sun is rising calm and bright ;
The birds are singing in the distant woods ;
Over his own sweet voice the Stock-dove broods ;
The Jay makes answer as the Magpie chatters ;
And all the air is filled with pleasant noise of waters.

II

All things that love the sun are out of doors ;
The sky rejoices in the morning's birth ;
The grass is bright with rain-drops ;—on the moors
The hare is running races in her mirth ;
And with her feet she from the plashy earth
Raises a mist ; that, glittering in the sun,
Runs with her all the way, wherever she doth run.

III

I was a Traveller then upon the moor ;
I saw the hare that raced about with joy ;
I heard the woods and distant waters roar ;
Or heard them not, as happy as a boy :
The pleasant season did my heart employ :
My old remembrances went from me wholly ;
And all the ways of men, so vain and melancholy.

IV

But, as it sometimes chanceth, from the might
Of joy in minds that can no further go,
As high as we have mounted in delight
In our dejection do we sink as low ;
To me that morning did it happen so ;
And fears and fancies thick upon me came ;
Dim sadness—and blind thoughts, I knew not, nor could
    name.

V

I heard the sky-lark warbling in the sky ;
And I bethought me of the playful hare :
Even such a happy Child of earth am I ;
Even as these blissful creatures do I fare ;
Far from the world I walk, and from all care ;
But there may come another day to me—
Solitude, pain of heart, distress, and poverty.

VI

My whole life I have lived in pleasant thought,
As if life's business were a summer mood ;
As if all needful things would come unsought
To genial faith, still rich in genial good ;
But how can He expect that others should
Build for him, sow for him, and at his call
Love him, who for himself will take no heed at all ?

VII

I thought of Chatterton, the marvellous Boy,
The sleepless Soul that perish'd in his pride ;
Of him who walk'd in glory and in joy
Following his plough, along the mountain-side :
By our own spirits are we deified :
We Poets in our youth begin in gladness ;
But thereof come in the end despondency and madness.

VI. He] cap. letter only denotes emphasis.   VII. him] Robert Burns.

VIII

Now, whether it were by peculiar grace,
A leading from above, a something given,
Yet it befell that, in this lonely place,
When I with these untoward thoughts had striven,
Beside a pool bare to the eye of heaven
I saw a Man before me unawares :
The oldest man he seem'd that ever wore grey hairs.

IX

As a huge stone is sometimes seen to lie
Couch'd on the bald top of an eminence ;
Wonder to all who do the same espy,
By what means it could thither come, and whence ;
So that it seems a thing endued with sense :
Like a sea-beast crawl'd forth, that on a shelf
Of rock or sand reposeth, there to sun itself ;

X

Such seem'd this Man, not all alive nor dead,
Nor all asleep—in his extreme old age :
His body was bent double, feet and head
Coming together in life's pilgrimage ;
As if some dire constraint of pain, or rage
Of sickness felt by him in times long past,
A more than human weight upon his frame had cast.

XI

Himself he propp'd, limbs, body, and pale face,
Upon a long grey staff of shaven wood :
And, still as I drew near with gentle pace,
Upon the margin of that moorish flood
Motionless as a cloud the old Man stood,
That heareth not the loud winds when they call ;
And moveth all together, if it move at all.

XII

At length, himself unsettling, he the pond
Stirr'd with his staff, and fixedly did look
Upon the muddy water, which he conn'd,
As if he had been reading in a book :
And now a stranger's privilege I took ;
And drawing to his side, to him did say,
' This morning gives us promise of a glorious day.'

XIII

A gentle answer did the old man make,
In courteous speech which forth he slowly drew :
And him with further words I thus bespake,
' What occupation do you there pursue ?
This is a lonesome place for one like you.'
Ere he replied, a flash of mild surprise
Broke from the sable orbs of his yet-vivid eyes.

XIV

His words came feebly, from a feeble chest,
But each in solemn order follow'd each,
With something of a lofty utterance drest—
Choice words and measured phrase, above the reach
Of ordinary men ; a stately speech,
Such as grave Livers do in Scotland use,
Religious men, who give to God and man their dues.

XV

He told, that to these waters he had come
To gather leeches, being old and poor :
Employment hazardous and wearisome !
And he had many hardships to endure :
From pond to pond he roam'd, from moor to moor ;
Housing, with God's good help, by choice or chance ;
And in this way he gain'd an honest maintenance.

XVI

The old Man still stood talking by my side ;
But now his voice to me was like a stream
Scarce heard ; nor word from word could I divide ;
And the whole body of the Man did seem
Like one whom I had met with in a dream ;
Or like a man from some far region sent,
To give me human strength, by apt admonishment.

XVII

My former thoughts return'd : the fear that kills ;
And hope that is unwilling to be fed ;
Cold, pain, and labour, and all fleshly ills ;
And mighty Poets in their misery dead.
Perplex'd, and longing to be comforted,
My question eagerly did I renew,
' How is it that you live, and what is it you do ? '

XVIII

He with a smile did then his words repeat ;
And said, that, gathering leeches, far and wide
He travell'd ; stirring thus about his feet
The waters of the pools where they abide.
' Once I could meet with them on every side ;
But they have dwindled long by slow decay ;
Yet still I persevere, and find them where I may.'

XIX

While he was talking thus, the lonely place,
The old Man's shape and speech—all troubled me :
In my mind's eye I seem'd to see him pace
About the weary moors continually,
Wandering about alone and silently.
While I these thoughts within myself pursued,
He, having made a pause, the same discourse renew'd.

XX

And soon with this he other matter blended,
Cheerfully utter'd with demeanour kind,
But stately in the main ; and when he ended,
I could have laugh'd myself to scorn to find
In that decrepit Man so firm a mind.
' God,' said I, ' be my help and stay secure :
I 'll think of the Leech-gatherer on the lonely moor ! '
Wordsworth.

189* *To Toussaint L'Ouverture*

TOUSSAINT, the most unhappy man of men !
Whether the whistling Rustic tend his plough
Within thy hearing, or thy head be now
Pillow'd in some deep dungeon's earless den ;—
O miserable Chieftain ! where and when
Wilt thou find patience ! Yet die not ; do thou
Wear rather in thy bonds a cheerful brow :
Though fallen thyself, never to rise again,
Live, and take comfort. Thou hast left behind
Powers that will work for thee ; air, earth, and skies ;
There 's not a breathing of the common wind
That will forget thee ; thou hast great allies ;
Thy friends are exultations, agonies,
And love, and man's unconquerable mind.
Wordsworth.

190 *King's College Chapel, Cambridge*

TAX not the royal Saint with vain expense,
    With ill-match'd aims the Architect who plann'd—
    Albeit labouring for a scanty band
    Of white-robed Scholars only—this immense

royal saint] King Henry VI.

And glorious Work of fine intelligence !
 Give all thou canst ; high Heaven rejects the lore
 Of nicely-calculated less or more ;
 So deem'd the man who fashion'd for the sense
These lofty pillars, spread that branching roof
 Self-poised, and scoop'd into ten thousand cells,
 Where light and shade repose, where music dwells
Lingering—and wandering on as loth to die ;
 Like thoughts whose very sweetness yieldeth proof
 That they were born for immortality.

Wordsworth.

191 *Abou Ben Adhem*

Abou Ben Adhem (may his tribe increase !)
Awoke one night from a deep dream of peace,
And saw, within the moonlight in his room,
Making it rich, and like a lily in bloom,
An angel writing in a book of gold :—
Exceeding peace had made Ben Adhem bold,
And to the presence in the room he said,
' What writest thou ? '—The vision raised its head,
And with a look made all of sweet accord,
Answer'd, ' The names of those that love the Lord.'
' And is mine one ? ' said Abou. ' Nay, not so,'
Replied the angel. Abou spoke more low,
But cheerly still ; and said, ' I pray thee, then,
Write me as one that loves his fellow men.'
The angel wrote and vanish'd. The next night
It came again with a great wakening light,
And show'd the names whom love of God had blest,
And lo ! Ben Adhem's name led all the rest.

Leigh Hunt.

192   *Christmas*

ALL after pleasures as I rid one day,
    My horse and I, both tired, body and mind,
With full cry of affections, quite astray,
    I took up in the next Inn I could find.

There when I came, whom found I but my dear,
    My dearest Lord, expecting till the grief
Of pleasures brought me to him, ready there
    To be all passengers' most sweet relief ?

O Thou, whose glorious yet contracted light,
    Wrapt in night's mantle, stole into a manger,
Since my dark soul and brutish is thy right,
    To Man of all beasts be not thou a stranger.

Furnish and deck my soul, that thou mayst have
A better lodging than a rack, or grave.
                         Herbert.

193   *On His Blindness*

WHEN I consider how my light is spent,
    Ere half my days, in this dark world and wide,
    And that one Talent which is death to hide
    Lodged with me useless, though my Soul more bent
To serve therewith my Maker, and present
    My true account, lest he returning chide,—
    Doth God exact day-labour, light deny'd ?
    I fondly ask : But patience, to prevent
That murmur, soon replies ; God doth not need
    Either man's work or his own gifts : who best
    Bear his mild yoke, they serve him best : His State

rack] manger, any wooden frame for cattle to pull fodder from.

Is Kingly ; Thousands at his bidding speed
And post o'er Land and Ocean without rest :
They also serve who only stand and wait.

Milton.

194*   *Paradise Lost*

Of Man's First Disobedience, and the Fruit
Of that Forbidden Tree, whose mortal taste
Brought Death into the World, and all our woe,
With loss of *Eden*, till one greater Man
Restore us, and regain the blissful Seat,
Sing Heav'nly Muse, that on the secret top
Of *Oreb*, or of *Sinai*, didst inspire
That Shepherd, who first taught the chosen Seed,
In the Beginning how the Heav'ns and Earth
Rose out of *Chaos* : or if *Sion* Hill   10
Delight thee more, and *Siloa's* Brook that flow'd
Fast by the Oracle of God ; I thence
Invoke thy aid to my advent'rous Song,
That with no middle flight intends to soar
Above th' *Aonian* Mount, while it pursues
Things unattempted yet in Prose or Rhyme.
And chiefly Thou, O Spirit, that dost prefer
Before all Temples th' upright heart and pure,
Instruct me, for Thou know'st ; Thou from the first
Wast present, and with mighty wings outspread 20
Dove-like sat'st brooding on the vast Abyss
And mad'st it pregnant : What in me is dark
Illumine, what is low raise and support ;
That to the highth of this great Argument
I may assert Eternal Providence,
And justify the ways of God to men.

16. rhyme] verse.   24. argument] subject-matter

Say first, for Heav'n hides nothing from thy view
Nor the deep tract of Hell, say first what cause
Moved our Grand Parents in that happy State,
Favour'd of Heav'n so highly, to fall off   30
From their Creator, and transgress his Will
For one restraint, Lords of the World besides ?
Who first seduced them to that foul revolt ?
Th' infernal Serpent ; he it was, whose guile
Stirr'd up with Envy and Revenge, deceived
The Mother of Mankind, what time his Pride
Had cast him out from Heav'n, with all his Host
Of Rebel Angels, by whose aid aspiring
To set himself in Glory above his Peers,
He trusted to have equal'd the most High,   40
If he opposed ; and with ambitious aim
Against the Throne and Monarchy of God
Raised impious War in Heav'n and Battle proud
With vain attempt. Him the Almighty Power
Hurl'd headlong flaming from th' Ethereal Sky
With hideous ruin and combustion down
To bottomless perdition, there to dwell
In Adamantine Chains and penal Fire,
Who durst defy th' Omnipotent to Arms.
Nine times the Space that measures Day and Night   50
To mortal men, he with his horrid crew
Lay vanquish'd, rolling in the fiery Gulf
Confounded though immortal : But his doom
Reserved him to more wrath ; for now the thought
Both of lost happiness and lasting pain
Torments him ; round he throws his baleful eyes
That witness'd huge affliction and dismay
Mix'd with obdúrate pride and stedfast hate :
At once as far as Angels ken he views
The dismal Situation waste and wild,   60
A Dungeon horrible on all sides round

41. he] that is Satan.

As one great Furnace flamed, yet from those flames
No light, but rather darkness visible
Served only to discover sights of woe,
Regions of sorrow, doleful shades, where peace
And rest can never dwell, hope never comes
That comes to all ; but torture without end
Still urges, and a fiery Deluge, fed
With ever-burning Sulphur unconsumed :
Such place Eternal Justice had prepared   70
For those rebellious, here their Prison ordain'd
In utter darkness, and their portion set
As far removed from God and light of Heav'n
As from the Centre thrice to th' utmost Pole.
O how unlike the place from whence they fell !
There the companions of his fall, o'erwhelm'd
With Floods and Whirlwinds of tempestuous fire,
He soon discerns, and welt'ring by his side
One next himself in power, and next in crime,
Long after known in *Palestine*, and named   80
Beëlzebub. To whom th' Arch-Enemy,
And thence in Heav'n call'd Satan, with bold words
Breaking the horrid silence thus began.

If thou beest he ; But O how fall'n ! how changed
From him, who in the happy Realms of Light
Clothed with transcendent brightness didst outshine
Myriads though bright : If he whom mutual league,
United thoughts and counsels, equal hope,
And hazard in the Glorious Enterprize,
Join'd with me once, now misery hath join'd   90
In equal ruin : into what Pit thou seest
From what highth fall'n, so much the stronger proved
He with his Thunder : and till then who knew
The force of those dire Arms ? yet not for those,
Nor what the Potent Victor in his rage
Can else inflict, do I repent or change
(Though changed in outward lustre) that fix'd mind,

And high disdain from sense of injured merit,
That with the Mightiest raised me to contend,
And to the fierce contention brought along   100
Innumerable force of Spirits arm'd
That durst dislike his reign, and me preferring,
His utmost power with adverse power opposed
In dubious Battle on the Plains of Heav'n,
And shook his throne. What though the field be lost ?
All is not lost ; the unconquerable Will,
And study of revenge, immortal hate,
And courage never to submit or yield :
And what is else not to be overcome ?
That Glory never shall his wrath or might   110
Extort from me.   To bow and sue for grace
With suppliant knee, and deify his power
Who from the terror of this Arm so late
Doubted his Empire, that were low indeed,
That were an ignominy and shame beneath
This downfall ; since by Fate the strength of Gods
And this Empýreal substance cannot fail,—
Since through experience of this great event
In Arms not worse, in foresight much advanced,
We may with more successful hope resolve   120
To wage by force or guile eternal War,
Irreconcilable to our grand Foe,
Who now triúmphs, and in th' excess of joy
Sole reigning holds the Tyranny of Heav'n.

So spake th' Apostate Angel, though in pain,
Vaunting aloud, but rack'd with deep despair :
And him thus answer'd soon his bold Compeer.

O Prince, O Chief of many Thronèd Powers,
That led th' imbattled Seraphim to War
Under thy conduct, and in dreadful deeds   130
Fearless, endanger'd Heav'n's perpetual King ;

117. empyreal] fiery ; epithet of the heavens.
130. conduct] leadership.

And put to proof his high Supremacy,
Whether upheld by strength, or Chance, or Fate ;
Too well I see and rue the dire event,
That with sad overthrow and foul defeat
Hath lost us Heav'n, and all this mighty Host
In horrible destruction laid thus low,
As far as Gods and Heav'nly Essences
Can perish : for the mind and spirit remains
Invincible, and vigour soon returns,   140
Though all our Glory extinct, and happy state
Here swallow'd up in endless misery.
But what if he our Conqueror (whom I now
Of force believe Almighty, since no less
Than such could have o'erpower'd such force as ours)
Have left us this our spirit and strength entire
Strongly to suffer and support our pains,
That we may so suffice his vengeful ire,
Or do him mightier service as his thralls
By right of War, whate'er his business be,   150
Here in the heart of Hell to work in Fire,
Or do his Errands in the gloomy Deep ?
What can it then avail though yet we feel
Strength undiminish'd, or eternal being
To undergo eternal punishment ?
Whereto with speedy words th' Arch-fiend reply'd.

    Fall'n Cherub, to be weak is miserable,
Doing or Suffering : but of this be sure,
To do ought good never will be our task,
But ever to do ill our sole delight,   160
As being the contrary to his high will
Whom we resist.   If then his Providence
Out of our evil seek to bring forth good,
Our labour must be to pervert that end,
And out of good still to find means of evil ;

157. cherub] Babylonian word for their winged Bull, symbol of
the sun-god.

Which ofttimes may succeed, so as perhaps
Shall grieve him, if I fail not, and disturb
His inmost counsels from their destined aim.
But see, the angry Victor hath recall'd
His Ministers of vengeance and pursuit   170
Back to the Gates of Heav'n : The Sulphurous Hail
Shot after us in storm, o'erblown hath laid
The fiery Surge, that from the Precipice
Of Heav'n received us falling ; and the Thunder,
Wing'd with red Lightning and impetuous rage,
Perhaps hath spent his shafts, and ceases now
To bellow through the vast and boundless Deep.
Let us not slip th' occasion, whether scorn,
Or satiate fury yield it from our Foe.
Seest thou yon dreary Plain, forlorn and wild,   180
The seat of desolation, void of light,
Save what the glimmering of these livid flames
Casts pale and dreadful ?   Thither let us tend
From off the tossing of these fiery waves,
There rest, if any rest can harbour there,
And reassembling our afflicted Powers,
Consult how we may henceforth most offend
Our Enemy, our own loss how repair,
How overcome this dire Calamity,
What reinforcement we may gain from Hope,   190
If not what resolution from despair. . . .

Milton.

195   *Satan's Kingdom*

    . . . Is this the Region, this the Soil, the Clime,
Said then the lost Archangel, this the seat
That we must change for Heav'n, this mournful gloom
For that celestial light ?   Be it so, since He

176. his] its, the thunder's.   187. offend in ure or annoy.

Who now is Sovran can dispose and bid
What shall be right : farthest from him is best,
Whom reason hath equal'd, force hath made supreme
Above his equals.   Farewell happy Fields
Where Joy for ever dwells : Hail horrors, hail
Infernal world, and thou profoundest Hell
Receive thy new Possessor ; One who brings
A mind not to be changed by Place or Time.
The mind is its own place, and in itself
Can make a Heav'n of Hell, a Hell of Heav'n.
What matter where, if I be still the same,
And what I should be, all but less than He
Whom Thunder hath made greater ?   Here at least
We shall be free ; th' Almighty hath not built
Here for his envy, will not drive us hence :
Here we may reign secure, and in my choice
To reign is worth ambition though in Hell :
Better to reign in Hell, than serve in Heav'n.
But wherefore let we then our faithful friends,
Th' associates and co-partners of our loss,
Lie thus astonish'd on th' oblivious Pool,
And call them not to share with us their part
In this unhappy Mansion, or once more
With rallied Arms to try what may be yet
Regain'd in Heav'n, or what more lost in Hell ?

Milton.

196

 THE expense of Spirit in a waste of shame
  Is lust in action ; and till action, lust
 Is perjured, murderous, bloody, full of blame,
  Savage, extreme, rude, cruel, not to trust ;

all but less] expression confusing 'only less than' and 'all but
equal to.'
oblivious] causing oblivion.

Enjoy'd no sooner but despisèd straight ;
Past reason hunted ; and no sooner had,
Past reason hated, as a swallow'd bait
On purpose laid to make the taker mad :
Mad in pursuit, and in possession so ;
Had, having, and in quest to have, extreme ;
A bliss in proof, and proved, a very woe ;
Before, a joy proposed ; behind, a dream.
    All this the world well knows ; yet none knows well
    To shun the heaven that leads men to this hell.

Shakespeare.

197   *Mercy*

From the Trial Scene in *The Merchant of Venice.*

PORTIA. Which is the merchant here, and which the
    Jew ?
DUKE. Antonio and old Shylock, both stand forth.
PORTIA. Is your name Shylock ?
SHYLOCK.   Shylock is my name.
PORTIA. Of a strange nature is the suit you follow ;
Yet in such rule that the Venetian law
Cannot impugn you as you do proceed.
You stand within his danger, do you not ?
    ANTONIO. Ay, so he says.
        PORTIA.   Do you confess the bond ?
    ANTONIO. I do.
PORTIA.   Then must the Jew be merciful.
SHYLOCK. On what compulsion must I ? tell me that.
    PORTIA. The quality of mercy is not strain'd,
It droppeth as the gentle rain from heaven
Upon the place beneath ; it is twice blest ;
It blesseth him that gives and him that takes :

but] than.

'Tis mightiest in the mightiest : it becomes
The thronèd monarch better than his crown ;
His sceptre shows the force of temporal power,
The attribute to awe and majesty,
Wherein doth sit the dread and fear of kings ;
But mercy is above this sceptred sway ;
It is enthronèd in the hearts of kings,
It is an attribute to God himself ;
And earthly power doth then show likest God's
When mercy seasons justice.   Therefore, Jew,
Though justice be thy plea, consider this,
That, in the course of justice, none of us
Should see salvation : we do pray for mercy ;
And that same prayer doth teach us all to render
The deeds of mercy.   I have spoke thus much
To mitigate the justice of thy plea ;
Which if thou follow, this strict court of Venice
Must needs give sentence 'gainst the merchant there.

SHYLOCK. My deeds upon my head ! I crave the law,
The penalty and forfeit of my bond. . . .

Shakespeare.

198

For Mercy, Courage, Kindness, Mirth,
There is no measure upon earth.
Nay, they wither, root and stem,
If an end be set to them.

Overbrim and overflow,
If your own heart you would know ;
For the spirit, born to bless,
Lives but in its own excess.

Laurence Binyon.

199   *Ministering Angels*

AND is there care in heaven ?   And is there love
In heavenly spirits to these creatures base,
That may compassion of their evils move ?
There is :—else much more wretched were the case
Of men than beasts.   But O ! th' exceeding grace
Of Highest God that loves his creatures so,
And all his works with mercy doth embrace,
That blessed Angels he sends to and fro
To serve to wicked man, to serve his wicked foe !

How oft do they their silver bowers leave,
To come to succour us that succour want !
How oft do they with golden pinions cleave
The flitting skies like flying pursuivant,
Against foul fiends to aid us militant !
They for us fight ; they watch and duly ward,
And their bright squadrons round about us plant ;
And all for love, and nothing for reward :
O ! why should heavenly God to man have such regard ?

                                  Spenser.*

200   *Prologue of the Attendant
Spirit in ' Comus '*

BEFORE the starry threshold of *Jove's* Court
My mansion is, where those immortal shapes
Of bright aëreal Spirits live insphered
In Regions mild of calm and sérene air,
Above the smoke and stir of this dim spot,
Which men call Earth, and, with low-thoughted care
Confined and pester'd in this pin-fold here,

insphered]*.

Strive to keep up a frail and feverish being,
Unmindful of the crown that Virtue gives
After this mortal change to her true Servants,
Amongst the enthron'd gods on sainted seats.
Yet some there be that by due steps aspire
To lay their just hands on that Golden Key
That opes the Palace of Eternity :
To such my errand is, and but for such
I would not soil these pure ambrosial weeds
With the rank vapours of this sin-worn mould. . . .

Milton.

201   *Satan's First Meeting with Death*

. . . Whence and what art thou, execrable shape,
That dar'st, though grim and terrible, advance
Thy miscreated Front athwart my way
To yonder Gates ? through them I mean to pass,—
That be assured, without leave ask'd of thee :
Retire, or taste thy folly, and learn by proof,
Hell-born, not to contend with Spirits of Heav'n.
  To whom the Goblin full of wrath reply'd,
Art thou that Traitor Angel, art thou he,
Who first broke peace in Heav'n and Faith, till then
Unbroken, and in proud rebellious Arms
Drew after him the third part of Heav'n's Sons,
Conjured against the highest, for which both Thou
And they, outcast from God, are here condemn'd
To waste Eternal days in woe and pain ?
And reckonest thou thyself with Spirits of Heav'n,
Hell-doom'd, and breath'st defiance here and scorn,
Where I reign King, and to enrage thee more,
Thy King and Lord ? Back to thy punishment,
False fugitive, and to thy speed add wings,

Lest with a whip of Scorpions I pursue
Thy ling'ring, or with one stroke of this Dart
Strange horror seize thee, and pangs unfelt before. . . .
                                        *Milton.**

202*   *The Fallen Angels*

. . . Others apart sat on a Hill retired,
In thoughts more elevate, and reason'd high
Of Providence, Foreknowledge, Will, and Fate,
Fix'd fate, free will, foreknowledge absolute,
And found no end, in wand'ring mazes lost.
Of good and evil much they argued then,
Of happiness and final misery,
Passion and apathy, and glory and shame,
Vain wisdom all, and false Philosophy :
Yet with a pleasing sorcery could charm   10
Pain for a while or anguish, and excite
Fallacious hope, or arm th' obdurèd breast
With stubborn patience as with triple steel.
Another part, in Squadrons and gross Bands
On bold adventure to discover wide
That dismal World, if any Clime perhaps
Might yield them easier habitation, bend
Four ways their flying march, along the banks
Of four infernal Rivers that disgorge
Into the burning Lake their baleful streams ;   20
Abhorrèd *Styx* the flood of deadly Hate,
Sad *Acheron* of Sorrow, black and deep ;
Cocytus, named of Lamentation loud
Heard on the rueful stream ; fierce *Phlegethon*
Whose waves of torrent fire inflame with Rage.
Far off from these a slow and silent stream,
Lethe the River of Oblivion rolls
Her watery Labyrinth, whereof who drinks

Forthwith his former state and being forgets,
Forgets both joy and grief, pleasure and pain.　　30
Beyond this flood a frozen Continent
Lies dark and wild, beat with perpetual storms
Of Whirlwind and dire Hail, which on firm land
Thaws not, but gathers heap, and ruin seems
Of ancient pile ;　all else deep snow and ice,
A gulf profound as that *Serbonian* Bog
Betwixt *Damiata* and mount *Casius* old,
Where Armies whole have sunk :　the parching Air
Burns frore, and cold performs th' effect of Fire.
Thither by harpy-footed Furies haled,　　40
At certain revolutions all the damn'd
Are brought :　and feel by turns the bitter change
Of fierce extremes, extremes by change more fierce,
From Beds of raging Fire to starve in Ice
Their soft Ethereal warmth, and there to pine
Immovable, infix'd, and frozen round,
Periods of time, thence hurried back to fire.
They ferry over this *Lethean* Sound
Both to and fro, their sorrow to augment,
And wish and struggle, as they pass, to reach　　50
The tempting stream, with one small drop to lose
In sweet forgetfulness all pain and woe,
All in one moment, and so near the brink ;
But fate withstands, and to oppose th' attempt
Medusa with *Gorgonian* terror guards
The Ford, and of itself the water flies
All taste of living wight, as once it fled
The lip of *Tantalus*.　Thus roving on
In confused march forlorn, th' advent'rous Bands
With shudd'ring horror pale, and eyes aghast　　60
View'd first their lamentable lot, and found
No rest :　through many a dark and dreary Vale
They pass'd, and many a Region dolorous,
O'er many a Frozen, many a Fiery Alp,

Rocks, Caves, Lakes, Fens, Bogs, Dens, and shades of
    death,
A Universe of death, which God by curse
Created evil, for evil only good,
Where all life dies, death lives, and nature breeds,
Perverse, all monstrous, all prodigious things,
Abominable, inutterable, and worse   70
Than Fables yet have feign'd, or fear conceived,
Gorgons and *Hydras*, and *Chimeras* dire. . .

                               Milton.

203   *Epilogue of 'Prometheus'*

.   .   .   .   .

ALL

Speak : thy strong words may never pass away.

DEMOGORGON

This is the day, which down the void abysm
At the Earth-born's spell yawns for Heaven's despotism,
   And Conquest is dragg'd captive through the deep :
Love, from its awful throne of patient power
In the wise heart, from the last giddy hour
   Of dread endurance, from the slippery, steep,
And narrow verge of crag-like agony, springs
And folds over the world its healing wings.

Gentleness, Virtue, Wisdom, and Endurance,
These are the seals of that most firm assurance
   Which bars the pit over Destruction's strength ;
And if, with infirm hand, Eternity,
Mother of many acts and hours, should free
   The serpent that would clasp her with his length ;
These are the spells by which to reassume
An empire o'er the disentangled doom.

To suffer woes which Hope thinks infinite ;
To forgive wrongs darker than death or night ;
  To defy Power, which seems omnipotent ;
To love, and bear ; to hope till Hope creates
From its own wreck the thing it contemplates ;
  Neither to change, nor falter, nor repent ;
This, like thy glory, Titan, is to be
Good, great and joyous, beautiful and free ;
This is alone Life, Joy, Empire, and Victory.
                         Shelley.

204   *New Year's Eve*

RING out, wild bells, to the wild sky,
    The flying cloud, the frosty light :
    The year is dying in the night ;
Ring out, wild bells, and let him die.

Ring out the old, ring in the new,
    Ring, happy bells, across the snow :
    The year is going, let him go ;
Ring out the false, ring in the true.

Ring out the grief that saps the mind,
    For those that here we see no more ;
    Ring out the feud of rich and poor,
Ring in redress to all mankind.

Ring out a slowly dying cause,
    And ancient forms of party strife ;
    Ring in the nobler modes of life,
With sweeter manners, purer laws.

        Titan] Prometheus.

Ring out the want, the care, the sin,
  The faithless coldness of the times ;
  Ring out, ring out my mournful rhymes,
But ring the fuller minstrel in.

Ring out false pride in place and blood,
  The civic slander and the spite ;
  Ring in the love of truth and right,
Ring in the common love of good.

Ring out old shapes of foul disease ;
  Ring out the narrowing lust of gold ;
  Ring out the thousand wars of old,
Ring in the thousand years of peace.

Ring in the valiant man and free,
  The larger heart, the kindlier hand ;
  Ring out the darkness of the land,
Ring in the Christ that is to be.
        Tennyson.

205   *Antiphon*

Cho. LET all the world in every corner sing,
   My God and King.

Vers. The heavens are not too high,
  His praise may thither fly :
  The earth is not too low,
  His praises there may grow.

Cho. Let all the world in every corner sing,
   My God and King.

Vers. The Church with psalms must shout,
  No door can keep them out :
  But above all, the heart
  Must bear the longest part.

Cho. Let all the world in every corner sing,
   My God and King.
      Herbert.

206   *Matins*

  I CANNOT ope mine eyes,
  But thou art ready there to catch
  My morning-soul and sacrifice ;
Then we must needs for that day make a match.

  My God, what is a heart ?
  Silver, or gold, or precious stone,
  Or star, or rainbow, or a part
Of all these things, or all of them in one ?

  My God, what is a heart,
  That thou shouldst it so eye, and woo,
  Pouring upon it all thy art,
As if that thou hadst nothing else to do ?

  Indeed, man's whole estate
  Amounts (and richly) to serve thee :
  He did not heaven and earth create,
Yet studies them, not Him by whom they be.

  Teach me thy love to know ;
  That this new light, which now I see,
  May both the work and workman show :
Then by a sunbeam I will climb to thee.
      Herbert.

207

O LIVING Will that shalt endure
    When all that seems shall suffer shock,
    Rise in the spiritual rock,
Flow thro' our deeds and make them pure,

That we may lift from out of dust
    A voice as unto him that hears,
    A cry above the conquer'd years
To one that with us works ; and trust.

With faith that comes of self-control,
    The truths that never can be proved ;
    Until we close with all we loved
And all we flow from, soul in soul.

Tennyson,

208   *The Song of Honour*

I CLIMB'D a hill as light fell short,
And rooks came home in scramble sort,
And fill'd the trees and flapp'd and fought
And sang themselves to sleep ;
An owl from nowhere with no sound
Swung by and soon was nowhere found,
I heard him calling half-way round,
Holloing loud and deep ;
A pair of stars, faint pins of light,
Then many a star, sail'd into sight,
And all the stars, the flower of night,
Were round me at a leap ;
To tell how still the valleys lay
I heard a watchdog miles away . . .
And bells of distant sheep.

I heard no more of bird or bell,
The mastiff in a slumber fell,
I stared into the sky,
As wondering men have always done
Since beauty and the stars were one,
Though none so hard as I.

It seem'd, so still the valleys were,
As if the whole world knelt at prayer,
Save me and me alone ;
So pure and wide that silence was
I fear'd to bend a blade of grass,
And there I stood like stone.

There, sharp and sudden, there I heard—
Ah ! some wild lovesick singing bird
Woke singing in the trees ?
The nightingale and babble-wren
Were in the English greenwood then,
And you heard one of these ?

The babble-wren and nightingale
Sang in the Abyssinian vale
That season of the year !
Yet, true enough, I heard them plain,
I heard them both again, again,
As sharp and sweet and clear
As if the Abyssinian tree
Had thrust a bough across the sea,
Had thrust a bough across to me
With music for my ear !

I heard them both, and Oh ! I heard
The song of every singing bird
That sings beneath the sky,
And with the song of lark and wren
The song of mountains, moths and men
And seas and rainbows vie !

I heard the universal choir,
The Sons of Light exalt their Sire
With universal song,
Earth's lowliest and loudest notes,
Her million times ten million throats
Exalt Him loud and long,
And lips and lungs and tongues of Grace
From every part and every place
Within the shining of His face,
The universal throng.

I heard the hymn of being sound
From every well of honour found
In human sense and soul :
The song of poets when they write
The testament of Beautysprite
Upon a flying scroll,
The song of painters when they take
A burning brush for Beauty's sake
And limn her features whole—

The song of men divinely wise
Who look and see in starry skies
Not stars so much as robins' eyes,
And when these pale away
Hear flocks of shiny pleiades
Among the plums and apple trees
Sing in the summer day—

The song of all both high and low
To some blest vision true,
The song of beggars when they throw
The crust of pity all men owe
To hungry sparrows in the snow,
Old beggars hungry too—
The song of kings of kingdoms when
They rise above their fortune men,
And crown themselves anew,—

The song of courage, heart and will
And gladness in a fight,
Of men who face a hopeless hill
With sparking and delight,
The bells and bells of song that ring
Round banners of a cause or king
From armies bleeding white—

The song of sailors every one
When monstrous tide and tempest run
At ships like bulls at red,
When stately ships are twirl'd and spun
Like whipping-tops and help there 's none
And mighty ships ten thousand ton
Go down like lumps of lead—

And song of fighters stern as they
At odds with fortune night and day,
Cramm'd up in cities grim and grey
As thick as bees in hives,
Hosannas of a lowly throng
Who sing unconscious of their song,
Whose lips are in their lives—

And song of some at holy war
With spells and ghouls more dread by far
Than deadly seas and cities are,
Or hordes of quarrelling kings—
The song of fighters great and small,
The song of pretty fighters all
And high heroic things—

The song of lovers—who knows how
Twitch'd up from place and time
Upon a sigh, a blush, a vow,
A curve or hue of cheek or brow,
Borne up and off from here and now
Into the void sublime !

And crying loves and passions still,
In every key from soft to shrill
And numbers never done,
Dog-loyalties to faith and friend,
And loves like Ruth's of old no end,
And intermission none—

And burst on burst for beauty and
For numbers not behind,
From men whose love of motherland
Is like a dog's for one dear hand,
Sole, selfless, boundless, blind—
And song of some with hearts beside
For men and sorrows far and wide,
Who watch the world with pity and pride
And warm to all mankind—

And endless joyous music rise
From children at their play,
And endless soaring lullabies
From happy, happy mothers' eyes,
And answering crows and baby cries,
How many who shall say !
And many a song as wondrous well
With pangs and sweets intolerable
From lonely hearths too gray to tell,
God knows how utter gray !
And song from many a house of care
When pain has forced a footing there
And there 's a Darkness on the stair
Will not be turn'd away—

And song—that song whose singers come
With old kind tales of pity from
The Great Compassion's lips,

That make the bells of Heaven to peal
Round pillows frosty with the feel
Of Death's cold finger tips—

The song of men all sorts and kinds,
As many tempers, moods and minds
As leaves are on a tree,
As many faiths and castes and creeds,
As many human bloods and breeds
As in the world may be ;

The song of each and all who gaze
On Beauty in her naked blaze,
Or see her dimly in a haze,
Or get her light in fitful rays
And tiniest needles even,
The song of all not wholly dark,
Not wholly sunk in stupor stark
Too deep for groping Heaven—

And alleluias sweet and clear
And wild with beauty men mis-hear,
From choirs of song as near and dear
To Paradise as they,
The everlasting pipe and flute
Of wind and sea and bird and brute,
And lips deaf men imagine mute
In wood and stone and clay,

The music of a lion strong
That shakes a hill a whole night long,
A hill as loud as he,
The twitter of a mouse among
Melodious greenery,
The ruby's and the rainbow's song,
The nightingale's—all three,

Q

The song of life that wells and flows
From every leopard, lark and rose
And everything that gleams or goes
Lack-lustre in the sea.

I heard it all, each, every note
Of every lung and tongue and throat,
Ay, every rhythm and rhyme
Of everything that lives and loves
And upward, ever upward moves
From lowly to sublime !
Earth's multitudinous Sons of Light,
I heard them lift their lyric might
With each and every chanting sprite
That lit the sky that wondrous night
As far as eye could climb !

I heard it all, I heard the whole
Harmonious hymn of being roll
Up through the chapel of my soul
And at the altar die,
And in the awful quiet then
Myself I heard, Amen, Amen,
Amen I heard me cry !
I heard it all and then although
I caught my flying senses, Oh,
A dizzy man was I !
I stood and stared ; the sky was lit,
The sky was stars all over it,
I stood, I knew not why,
Without a wish, without a will,
I stood upon that silent hill
And stared into the sky until
My eyes were blind with stars and still
I stared into the sky.

Ralph Hodgson.

209*

Man, one harmonious soul of many a soul,
  Whose nature is its own divine control,
Where all things flow to all, as rivers to the sea ;
  Familiar acts are beautiful through love ;
  Labour, and pain, and grief, in life's green grove
Sport like tame beasts, none knew how gentle they
      could be !

His will, with all mean passions, bad delights,
  And selfish cares, its trembling satellites,
A spirit ill to guide, but mighty to obey,
  Is as a tempest-wingèd ship, whose helm
  Love rules, through waves which dare not overwhelm,
Forcing life's wildest shores to own its sovereign sway.

All things confess his strength. Through the cold mass
  Of marble and of colour his dreams pass ;
Bright threads whence mothers weave the robes their
      children wear ;
  Language is a perpetual Orphic song,
  Which rules with Dædal harmony a throng
Of thoughts and forms, which else senseless and shape-
      less were.

The lightning is his slave ; heaven's utmost deep
  Gives up her stars, and like a flock of sheep
They pass before his eye, are number'd, and roll on !
  The tempest is his steed, he strides the air ;
  And the abyss shouts from her depth laid bare,
Heaven, hast thou secrets ? Man unveils me ; I have
      none.

                                        Shelley.

210

> . . . He either fears his fate too much,
>   Or his deserts are small,
> That dares not put it to the touch,
>   To gain or lose it all. . . .
>
> <div align="right"><i>Montrose.</i>*</div>

211   *Sacramentum Supremum*

Ye that with me have fought and fail'd and fought
  To the last desperate trench of battle's crest,
Not yet to sleep, not yet ; our work is nought ;
  On that last trench the fate of all may rest.
Draw near, my friends ; and let your thoughts be high ;
  Great hearts are glad when it is time to give ;
Life is no life to him that dares not die,
  And death no death to him that dares to live.

Draw near together ; none be last or first ;
  We are no longer names, but one desire ;
With the same burning of the soul we thirst,
  And the same wine to-night shall quench our fire.
Drink ! to our fathers who begot us men,
  To the dead voices that are never dumb ;
Then to the land of all our loves, and then
  To the long parting, and the age to come.

Henry Newbolt.

212*

Now, God be thank'd Who has match'd us with His hour,
  And caught our youth, and waken'd us from sleeping,
With hand made sure, clear eye, and sharpen'd power,
  To turn, as swimmers into cleanness leaping,

Glad from a world grown old and cold and weary,
    Leave the sick hearts that honour could not move,
And half-men, and their dirty songs and dreary,
    And all the little emptiness of love !

Oh ! we who have known shame, we have found release
        there,
    Where there 's no ill, no grief, but sleep has mending,
    Nought broken save this body, lost but breath ;
Nothing to shake the laughing heart's long peace there
    But only agony, and that has ending ;
    And the worst friend and enemy is but Death.

                                        Brooke.

213

        No coward soul is mine,
    No trembler in the world's storm-troubled sphere :
        I see Heaven's glories shine,
    And faith shines equal, arming me from fear.

        O God within my breast,
    Almighty, ever-present Deity !
        Life—that in me has rest,
    As I—undying Life—have power in Thee !

        Vain are the thousand creeds
    That move men's hearts, unutterably vain,
        Worthless as wither'd weeds
    Or idle froth amid the boundless main,

        To waken doubt in one
    Holding so fast by Thine infinity ;
        So surely anchor'd on
    The steadfast rock of immortality.

With wide-embracing love
Thy spirit animates eternal years,
Pervades and broods above,
Changes, sustains, dissolves, creates and rears.

Though earth and man were gone,
And suns and universes ceased to be,
And Thou were left alone,
Every existence would exist in Thee.

There is not room for Death,
Nor atom that his might could render void :
Thou—THOU art Being and Breath,
And what THOU art may never be destroyed.

Emily Brontë.

214   *Content*

ART thou poor, yet hast thou golden slumbers ?
          O sweet content !
Art thou rich, yet is thy mind perplex'd ?
          O punishment !
Dost thou laugh to see how fools are vex'd
To add to golden numbers golden numbers ?
O sweet content ! O sweet, O sweet content !
     Work apace, apace, apace, apace ;
     Honest labour bears a lovely face ;
Then hey nonny nonny—hey nonny nonny !

Canst drink the waters of the crispèd spring ?
          O sweet content !
Swimm'st thou in wealth, yet sink'st in thine own tears ?
          O punishment !
Then he that patiently Want's burden bears
No burden bears, but is a king, a king !

O sweet content! O sweet, O sweet content!
  Work apace, apace, apace, apace;
  Honest labour bears a lovely face;
Then hey nonny nonny—hey nonny nonny.

Dekker.

215   *The Soul's Pilgrimage*

GIVE me my scallop-shell of quiet,
My staff of faith to walk upon,
My scrip of joy, immortal diet,
My bottle of salvation,
My gown of glory, hope's true gage;
And thus I 'll take my pilgrimage.

Blood must be my body's balmer;
No other balm will there be given;
Whilst my soul, like quiet palmer,
Travelleth towards the land of heaven;
  Over the silver mountains,
  Where spring the nectar fountains:
    There will I kiss
    The bowl of bliss,
And drink mine everlasting fill
Upon every milken hill.
My soul will be a-dry before;
But, after, it will thirst no more.

Raleigh.

216* *The Character of a Happy Life*

How happy is he born and taught
  That serveth not another's will;
Whose armour is his honest thought,
  And simple truth his utmost skill!

scallop-shell] see No. 15.   scrip] almsbag.   gage] pledge.
balmer] embalmer.   palmer] pilgrim.

Whose passions not his masters are ;
  Whose soul is still prepared for death,
Untied unto the world with care
  Of prince's love or vulgar breath. . . .

Who hath his life from rumours freed ;
  Whose conscience is his strong retreat ;
Whose state can neither flatterers feed,
  Nor ruin make accusers great :

Who God doth late and early pray
  More of his grace than gifts to lend ;
And entertains the harmless day
  With a well-chosen book or friend :

This man is free from servile bands
  Of hope to rise, or fear to fall ;
Lord of himself, though not of lands ;
  And having nothing, he hath all.

Wotton.

217* *Constancy*

    Who is the honest man ?
He that doth still and strongly good pursue,
To God, his neighbour, and himself most true :
    Whom neither force nor fawning can
Unpin, or wrench from giving all their due :

    Whose honesty is not
So loose or easy, that a ruffling wind
Can blow away, or glittering look it blind :
    Who rides his sure and even trot,
While the world now rides by, now lags behind :

Who, when great trials come,
Nor seeks, nor shuns them ; but doth calmly stay
Till he the thing and the example weigh :
All being brought into a sum,
What place or person calls for, he doth pay :

Whom none can work or woo
To use in any thing a trick or sleight ;
For above all things he abhors deceit :
His words and works and fashion too
All of a piece are, all are clear and straight :

Who never melts or thaws
At close temptations : when the day is done,
His goodness sets not, but in dark can run ;
The sun to others writeth laws,
And is their Virtue ; Virtue is his Sun :

Who, when he is to treat
With sick folks, women, those whom passions sway,
Allows for that, and keeps his constant way :
Whom others' faults do not defeat ;
But though men fail him, yet his part doth play :

Whom nothing can procure,
When the wide world runs bias, from his will
To writhe his limbs, and share, not mend the ill :—
This is the Marksman, safe and sure,
Who still is right, and prays to be so still.

Herbert.

218 *Character of the Happy Warrior*

Who is the happy Warrior ?   Who is he
That every man in arms should wish to be ?

—It is the generous Spirit, who, when brought
Among the tasks of real life, hath wrought

Upon the plan that pleased his boyish thought :
Whose high endeavours are an inward light
That makes the path before him always bright :
Who, with a natural instinct to discern
What knowledge can perform, is diligent to learn ;
Abides by this resolve, and stops not there,
But makes his moral being his prime care ;
Who, doom'd to go in company with Pain,
And Fear, and Bloodshed, miserable train !
Turns his necessity to glorious gain ;
In face of these doth exercise a power
Which is our human nature's highest dower ;
Controls them and subdues, transmutes, bereaves
Of their bad influence, and their good receives :
By objects, which might force the soul to abate
Her feeling, render'd more compassionate ;
Is placable—because occasions rise
So often that demand such sacrifice ;
More skilful in self-knowledge, even more pure,
As tempted more ; more able to endure,
As more exposed to suffering and distress ;
Thence, also, more alive to tenderness.
—'Tis he whose law is reason ; who depends
Upon that law as on the best of friends ;
Whence, in a state where men are tempted still
To evil for a guard against worse ill,
And what in quality or act is best
Doth seldom on a right foundation rest,
He labours good on good to fix, and owes
To virtue every triumph that he knows :
—Who, if he rise to station of command,
Rises by open means ; and there will stand
On honourable terms, or else retire,
And in himself possess his own desire :
Who comprehends his trust, and to the same
Keeps faithful with a singleness of aim ;

And therefore does not stoop, nor lie in wait
For wealth, or honours, or for worldly state :
Whom they must follow ; on whose head must fall,
Like showers of manna, if they come at all :
Whose powers shed round him in the common strife,
Or mild concerns of ordinary life,
A constant influence, a peculiar grace ;
But who, if he be call'd upon to face
Some awful moment to which Heaven has join'd
Great issues, good or bad for human kind,
Is happy as a Lover ; and attired
With sudden brightness, like a Man inspired ;
And, through the heat of conflict, keeps the law
In calmness made, and sees what he foresaw ;
Or if an unexpected call succeed,
Come when it will, is equal to the need :
—He who, though thus endued as with a sense
And faculty for storm and turbulence,
Is yet a Soul whose master-bias leans
To homefelt pleasures and to gentle scenes ;
Sweet images ! which, wheresoe'er he be,
Are at his heart ; and such fidelity
It is his darling passion to approve ;
More brave for this, that he hath much to love :—
'Tis, finally, the Man, who, lifted high,
Conspicuous object in a Nation's eye,
Or left unthought-of in obscurity,—
Who, with a toward or untoward lot,
Prosperous or adverse, to his wish or not—
Plays, in the many games of life, that one
Where what he most doth value must be won :
Whom neither shape of danger can dismay,
Nor thought of tender happiness betray :
Who, not content that former worth stand fast,
Looks forward, persevering to the last,
From well to better, daily self-surpass'd :

Who, whether praise of him must walk the earth
For ever, and to noble deeds give birth,
Or he must fall, to sleep without his fame,
And leave a dead unprofitable name—
Finds comfort in himself and in his cause ;
And, while the mortal mist is gathering, draws
His breath in confidence of Heaven's applause :

This is the happy Warrior ; this is He
That every Man in arms should wish to be.
Wordsworth, 1805.

219   *Maxims*

By all means use sometimes to be alone.
Salute thyself ; see what thy soul doth wear.
Dare to look in thy chest, for 'tis thine own ;
And tumble up and down what thou find'st there.
    Who cannot rest till he good fellows find,
      He breaks up house, turns out of doors his mind.

Be thrifty, but not covetous ; therefore give
Thy need, thine honour, and thy friend his due.
Never was scraper brave man.   Get to live ;
Then live, and use it : else it is not true
    That thou hast gotten.   Surely Use alone
      Makes money not a cóntemptible stone.

Yet in thy thriving still misdoubt some evil ;
Lest gaining gain on thee, and make thee dim
To all things else.   Wealth is the conjurer's devil ;
Whom when he thinks he hath, the devil hath him.
    Gold thou mayst safely touch ; but if it stick
      Unto thy hands, it woundeth to the quick.

What skills it, if a bag of stones or gold
About thy neck do drown thee ? Raise thy head;
Take stars for money ; stars not to be told
By any art, yet to be purchasèd.
  None is so wasteful as the scraping dame :
  She loseth three for one ; her soul, rest, fame.

Laugh not too much : the witty man laughs least;
For wit is news only to ignorance.
Less at thine own things laugh ; lest in the jest
Thy person share, and the conceit advance :
  Make not thy sport abuses ; for the fly
  That feeds on dung is colourèd thereby.

Pick out of mirth, like stones out of thy ground,
Profaneness, filthiness, abusiveness.
These are the scum with which coarse wits abound ;
The fine may spare these well, yet not go less.
  All things are big with jest : nothing that 's plain
  But may be witty, if thou hast the vein.

Envy not greatness ; for thou mak'st thereby
Thyself the worse, and so the distance greater :
Be not thine own worm : yet such jealousy,
As hurts not others but may make thee better,
  Is a good spur.   Correct thy passion's spite ;
  Then may the beasts draw thee to happy light.

Be calm in arguing ; for fierceness makes
Error a fault, and truth discourtesy.
Why should I feel another man's mistakes
More than his sicknesses or poverty ?
  In love I should : but anger is not love,
  Nor wisdom neither ; therefore gently move.

Be useful where thou livest, that they may
Both want and wish thy pleasing presence still.
Kindness, good parts, great places are the way
To compass this. Find out men's wants and will,
 And meet them there. All worldly joys go less
 To the one joy of doing kindnesses.

Sum up at night what thou hast done by day ;
And in the morning, what thou hast to do.
Dress and undress thy soul : mark the decay
And growth of it : if with thy watch, that too
 Be down, then wind up both. Since we shall be
 Most surely judged, make thy accounts agree.

In brief, acquit thee bravely ; play the man.
Look not on pleasures as they come, but go.
Defer not the least virtue : life's poor span
Make not an ell by trifling in thy woe.
 If thou do ill, the joy fades, not the pains :
 If well, the pain doth fade, the joy remains.

Herbert.

NOTES

The numeration, in thicker type, refers to the poems and not to pages.

2. *springs . . . that lies.* 'The northern Early English 3rd person plur. in *-s* is extremely common in the Folio Shakespeare. In some cases the subject-noun may be considered as singular in *thought.*'—*Abbott. Shakesp. Gram.*

34. *silent moves the feet.* See note on **2.** Blake was probably influenced by Shakespeare's use. Three stanzas omitted at end.

38. From a long ode 'To the immortal memory and friendship of that noble pair, Sir Lucius Cary [Lord Falkland, who fell at Naseby, 1640] and Sir Henry Morison.'

39. An extract from *Auguries of Innocence.*

40. Stanza III. *the turning sphere.* 'Sphere' in the older poets implies the ancient Ptolemaic system of astronomy, in which ten spheres circle round the earth, carrying the Sun, the Moon, the seven planets, and the fixed stars. The sphere was a spinning shell of undefined substance carrying the planet : they made music by their motion. See stanza XIII., and note on **96.**—VI. *Lucifer,* the morning star.—VIII. *Pan,* the god of Nature, here for the Lord of all.—X. *Cynthia,* the moon. Her *hollow round,* see note on stanza III.—XXI. *Lars and Lemures* [pronounce *Lĕmmurs,* Englished from *Larēs and Lemurēs*], the household gods and spirits of the dead.—*Flamens,* Roman priests.—XXII. *twice-batter'd god,* Dagon.—*Ashtaroth* (Astarte), Phœnician goddess, later identified with Venus.—*Hammon,* Ammon, an Ethiopian god worshipped widely in N. Africa under the form of a ram.—*Thammuz,* Tammus, an obscure Asiatic deity identified with Adonis, whose myth represented the death of the year in winter.—XXIV. *Osiris,* Egyptian god of Agriculture, probably confused here with the sacred Bull, Apis.—XXV. *Typhon,* a primitive Greek monster-god, father of the Winds.—XXVI. *Fays,* fairies.

41. A selection from sixty similar stanzas in *Christmas Antiphons.*

44. Attempts by Swinburne, Rossetti, Yeats, and other

editors to harmonise the fragmentary phrases of this mag-
nificent poem have failed. Its force is not impaired by the
irregularities of verbal structure. I give John Sampson's con-
servative text.

48. Part II. stanza 4. *'Twas right, said they.* The marginal
gloss appended by Coleridge to later editions explains that
the Mariner's shipmates here make themselves accomplices in
his crime: And, in Part III. stanza 11, *I've won* means that
'Life-in-Death winneth the Mariner from Death.'—Part VII.
stanza 3. *I trow.* This pronunciation rhyming with *now* is an
example of an obsolete word wrongly spoken. *Trow* rhymes
with *owe*, etc. : thus,

> 'Have more than thou showest,
> Speak less than thou knowest,
> Lend less than thou owest,
> Ride more than thou goest,
> Learn more than thou trowest,
> Set less than thou throwest.'—*King Lear*, i. 4.

52. This section of a poem, which Shelley subsequently
altered and divided up, stands (as given here) metrically apart
from the rest.

56. *Martinmas.* The feast of St. Martin, the 'Apostle of
Gaul,' commemorated as a lesser Saint in the English Church
on Nov. 11th, which is now Armistice Day. St. Martin was
a soldier, son of a military tribune in the army of the emperor
Constantine in the fourth century. From early youth he was
a convert to Christianity and became Bishop of Tours, where
his memory is perpetuated. He is usually represented in the
act of dividing his cloak with his sword in order to bestow
half of it on a naked beggar.

60. The last ten lines are from a longer poem by *Lieut.
Hinches.* Burns made his song of them. Hinches' spellings,
love and *well*, do not forbid dialectal pronunciation.

63. Attributed to *Capt. Ogilvie,* and appears in Scott's
Rokeby quoted in the notes. The text here is Burns's version
of it.

68. Part of a Jacobite song adapted by Burns.

69. *fool,* an unfortunate rhyme because its initial suggests
fowl. The last couplet has become proverbial, with *and* in
place of *or,* as if it meant 'the rest is all rubbish.' Pope
meant that the rest was only clothes, in the cobbler his leather
apron, in the parson his stuff gown. The juxtaposition of *all*

with *but*, when *but* means *nothing but*, is only excused by the regular accent of the verse, which forbids the usual meaning of the common phrase *all bùt*.

70. In 4th stanza *guid faith* is an exclamation.

72. Founded on a traditional Cornish song.

73. Observe the unmatched accumulative value of the refrain : also that the lingo is the narrator's, not the captain's.

75. Byron sent this to John Murray, the publisher, as a jocular draft of his reply to Dr. Polidori on reading that author's play. That the personages who figure in this society are not all known to us does not weaken the humour of the picture. On p. 92 the two ejaculation-marks in third and fourth lines from foot are added by present editor.

76. Many of Pope's lines have passed into common speech: this extract contains examples.

85. Translated from the Greek of Moschus.

89. *Ixion's wheel.* Ixion was king of the Lapithæ, who fought with the Centaurs. As punishment for his crimes and ingratitude to Zeus he was chained to a fiery wheel which revolved for ever in the lower world.—*Memphian Sphinx.* Sphinx was a monstrous being in Greek mythology, with a woman's head on the body of a winged lion. In Egypt, whence it was derived, it was a couchant (unwinged) lion, human in form from the breast upwards ; and rows of these mysterious figures lined the avenues of the temples. Memphis was one of the earliest historical cities in Egypt and had magnificent temples. The famous colossal Sphinx is by the Pyramids at Gizeh, which is some miles down the Nile from Memphis.

96. Lorenzo is talking with Jessica (*Merch. of Ven.* Act v.) ; an example of the lyrical beauty which Shakespeare introduces into his blank verse.—*Like an angel sings*, see note on 40, stanza III. Plato says, 'On the upper surface of each sphere is a Siren, who goes round with them, hymning a single sound and note.'

105. *Lay of the Last Minstrel.* Opening of last canto.

106. The comparison is between Tuscany and Yorkshire : *Lavernia* (La Verna, Alvernia), where St. Francis received the stigmata, in the Apennines above Florence, ' Nel crudo sasso intra Tevere ed Arno,' Dante, *Par.* XI. t. 36.—*Scargill* is part of the scene of Scott's *Rokeby*.

108. The opening of *Endymion*, published 1818.

R

110. *The Spirit of the Sphere,* omitting the invocations.

121. From a sonnet in the *Arcadia,* omitting 5 lines.

122. The famous last stanza of Lovelace's lyric, *When Love with unconfinèd wings.* The other three are unworthy of it.

129. *Sérene lights.* This ' recession of accent,' where two strong speech-accents collide, was an old habit of speech, now lost. It is frequent in Shakespeare ; Milton renounced it in his later work ; Shelley rather affected it, and his practice decides the accent here.

130. l. 15. *Sisters,* the Muses who frequented the fount on Mt. Parnassus.—23. *hill,* in pastoral imagery, the University of Cambridge.—36. *Damœtas,* a shepherd, here for some Cambridge poet.—54. *Mona high,* Anglesey, then wooded ; it has, however, no 'heights.' Holyhead is perhaps intended. —55. *Deva,* the Dee, a river with magical legends. These places are near the scene of the wreck.—58. *Orpheus,* in the Greek legend torn to pieces by Thracian women.—75. *blind Fury,* Atropos, one of the three Fates.—77. *Ears.* The ear regarded as the seat of memory (Conington).—85. *Arethuse,* a stream in Sicily, the land of Theocritus ; *Mincius,* by Virgil's birthplace : those being the two pastoral poets in whose manner this poem is written.—96. *Hippotades,* Æolus, the god of the winds.—99. *Panopë,* one of the fifty Nereids, perhaps here representing by her name the calm sea and wide horizon (Palgrave).—103. *Camus,* the river-god of Cambridge.—106. *inscribed with woe,* a Greek fancy that the petals were marked with AI. Apollo had accidentally killed the youth Hyacinthos with a quoit, and the plant sprang up from his blood.—109. *Pilot,* of the church, St. Peter. Milton here condemns the corrupt clergy.—132. *Alpheus,* the river-lover of Arethusa. In the strange legend their waters mixed, and are here identified : the *return* is to the subject of the monody. —160. *Bellerus,* Milton's invention of a ' name-father' for Land's End, which was called Bellerium.—161. *Vision.* Original text has no capital initial ; but the vision is the Archangel Michael, who appeared on St. Michael's Mount.—162. *Namancos and Bayona,* places in Spain due south of Land's End.

135. Coleridge's *Christabel* is an unfinished poem.

137. *Childe Harold,* iv. stanzas 140-1.

140. *demesne.* The Anglo-French spelling of the law-books ; the prevailing pronunciation of the final syllable is as

in the rhyme here; but is in good legal and general use pro-
nounced as in its variant form *domain*; and this is historically
preferable (*O.E.D.*). Note also the homophone *demean* in
common use.

143. *Proteus*, the prophetic ' old man of the Sea,' a person-
age rich in delightful legends.—*Triton*, a son of Poseidon and
Amphitrite, who lived in a garden under the sea : usually
represented with a dolphin's tail. Tritons are often imagined
as numerous as Mermaids.

145. An unfinished poem of which the first two stanzas are
given.

147. *Tempe*, a beautiful mountain gorge in Thessaly con-
nected with the worship of Apollo.

148. Last stanza of three.

151. On occasion, when the length of this poem is incon-
venient, the bracketed stanzas can be omitted.

154. Last stanza omitted. In st. 1, *winds, birds*, and *floods*
are all genitives, and *birds* is plural. Accidence ambiguous.

155. Note *Day* is fem. in stanza 2, masc. in 3.

156. *Hippocrene*. A fountain on Mt. Helicon sacred to the
Muses, fabled to have sprung up from a stroke of Pegasus'
hoof, Ἵππου κρήνη. The English word is always a trisyllable.

159. *fast* is used for ' swiftly ' in stanza 4, and five lines
above for ' firm.' In first stanza *tir'd* is a disyllable = *tierd*.

171. Fourteen lines of fanciful mythology are omitted as
indicated in numeration. l. 10. *Morpheus*, the god of dreams.
—59. *Cynthia*, the moon.—88. *Hermes*, a mythical king of
Egypt named Thot, to whom the Neo-Platonists ascribed the
name and universal wisdom of the Greek god Hermes. He
is *thrice-great* as King, Priest, and Philosopher (Browne).—
89. The spirits of the dead are imagined as inhabiting the
starry ' spheres ' : see note on 40.—104. *Musæus, i.e.* to recall
the lost poems of Musæus, and the song by which Orpheus
rescued Eurydice from Hell, and the tale that Chaucer left
unfinished.—134. *Sylvan*, the forest-god.

172. *Maian*. The Greek Maia was mother of Hermes. The
Latin goddess of that name became associated with the month
of May, when also Hermes' (Mercury's) feast was kept. Hence
perhaps the rare epithet ' Maian ' here may mean ' scented
like spring flowers.' Compare ' the incense of all flowers '
just above.

175. l. 10. *Cimmerian.* The Cimmerians lived at the end of the world where the sun never shone.—29. *Hebe,* cup-bearer of the Gods.—125. *Hymen,* god of marriage, commonly represented in English masques as here described (Browne).—136. *Lydian airs,* the ecclesiastical Mode which in the seventeenth century was equivalent to our scale of F major.—150. *Eurydice.* The story half told in **171,** l. 104.

176. From *Sleep and Poetry.* A good example of Keats's objective style. 'These images are of life considered first as a mere atomic movement in a general flux, then as a dream on the brink of destruction, then as a budding hope, then as an intellectual distraction, then as an ecstatic glimpse of beauty, and lastly as an instinctive pleasure.'—*Montmorenci,* the river in Canada.

178. From *As you like it,* ii. 7. *his sound, i.e.* its sound, referring to *voice.* Its, the genitive of it, is not found before Elizabethan writers; 'his' was the old genitive, and is much more frequent than 'its' in Shakespeare.

179. From the *Essay on Man,* end of Ep. ii.—l. 2. *will change,* we should say *would change.*—l. 16. *tickled with a straw*: as this is not peculiar to babes, the expression must be metaphorical, and its apparent force immediately disappears. —Four lines below, in *beads and prayer-books,* the cynicism is overdone.

182. From *Tintern Abbey.*

183. *Essay on Man,* beginning of Ep. ii.

188. Title of this poem is *Resolution and Independence.*

189. François Dominique Toussaint, surnamed L'Ouverture, was governor of St. Domingo, and chief of the African slaves enfranchised by the decree of the French Convention (1794). He resisted Napoleon's edict re-establishing slavery in St. Domingo, was arrested and sent to Paris in June 1802, and there died after ten months' imprisonment in April 1803 (Hutchinson).

194. l. 11. *Siloa's brook,* Pool of Siloam.—12. *fast by,* hard by, near by, not 'swift.'—15. *Aonian Mount,* Helicon, the abode of Apollo and the Muses.—92. *highth,* always thus, pronounced as spelt, in Milton.—109. 'This question is parenthetical; it means, the true glory is to be unconquered in spirit, though the field be lost' (Beeching).

199. From *The Faery Queen,* opening of 8th canto of Bk. ii.

200. l. 3. *insphered.* See note to **171**, l. 89.

201. *P.L.* Bk. II. 681.

202. *P.L.* Bk. II. 557. l. 55. *Medusa,* one of the three Gorgons, whose head, with snakes for hair, turned him who looked on it into stone.

209. The last four stanzas of nine in one of the lyrical monodies spoken by Earth in the last Act of *Prometheus.*

210. The second half of the second stanza of four.

212. Inspired by the call of the Great War.

216. Text of this poem is based on what would seem the best authority among many variants, some of which are probably the author's own corrections. One stanza is omitted on account of its perplexed grammar :

> ' *Who envieth none that chance doth raise,*
> *Or vice; who never understood*
> *How deepest wounds are given by praise;*
> *Nor rules of state, but rules of good.*'

217. In the last line of stanza 4 I have substituted *are* for *and* in the common text : *All of a piece, and all are clear and straight*; and in last stanza *Marksman* for *Markman.*—In l. 13, *the thing and the example* means ' the principle and its spiritual application ' (Palmer).

INDEX OF AUTHORS

262

INDEX OF FIRST LINES

EXPLANATION OF REFERENCES,
ETC.

THE FOOTNOTES.

These are primarily a glossary of obsolete or dialectal words set where a reader may find their meaning without turning the pages. This convenience is sometimes used for difficulties of a similar scale.

GENERAL NOTES.

Wherever an asterisk [*] occurs in the text, whether at the number or title or ascription of a poem, it refers to the Notes at the end, pp. 255-261 : and when there is no asterisk to a poem, there is no note to it.

In compiling these annotations—which are explanatory of allusions and obscurities of all kinds—the experience and industry of previous commentators has been freely drawn upon ; but where no authority is named it may be assumed that the information is derived from common sources. All critical remarks have a merely educational intention.

TEXT.

Care has been taken to collate the best texts and to provide the best readings. This is not always easy, and the publishers will be grateful for notification of any mistakes or errors. The text of Milton has been expressly attended to. It is the original text (from Dean Beeching's edition) with only such convenient alterations of the spelling as are free from all scholarly objection. The original italicising of proper names and initialing of important words with capitals has been kept, as being of æsthetic value, and generally making the reading of the poem easier. In the few cases where the capitals have been changed the conditions were specially considered.

ORDER.

While there is a general scheme of having the simpler poems at the beginning of the book and the more difficult ones towards the end, this order of simplicity has often been set aside in the disposition of the subject-matter, on the grouping and sequence of which the pleasantness and companionable character of the book must depend.

CHOICE.

The extracts from Milton are no longer than is profitable in an educational book ; since he is not only our best link backwards with Chaucer, but his serene mastery, economy, and dignity make him the most useful model for all young students. His verse is therefore very good for learning by heart and for elementary recitation. Some other poems were chosen also for their usefulness in recitation.

In a book of this kind the older writers have a far stronger claim than the later ; since it is essential that students should have a good acquaintance with what must always be the foundation of our living literature. It is true that we overlook or condone blemishes in the old poems, while we are critical or intolerant towards faults of similar or less magnitude in contemporaries : and this must be so, because the older poems have passed their ordeal and won their place. It is by setting old and new together that the latter will win the same privilege. The Editor offers this attempt with due deference, and has to thank many friends for the ready assistance of their judgment.   R. B.